Top 25 locator map

TwinPack
Provence &
the Côte d'Azur

TERESA FISHER

Teresa Fisher is an experienced travel writer, confirmed Francophile and author of numerous AA publications including *Essential French Riviera, CityPacks Munich* and *Amsterdam*, and *Spiral Guides to Paris, Florence* and *Dublin*.

If you have any comments or suggestions for this guide you can contact the editor at *Twinpacks@theAA.com*

AA Publishing
Find out more about AA Publishing and the wide range of travel publications and services the AA provides by visiting our website at *www.theAA.com/travel*

Contents

About this book

TwinPack Provence & the Côte d'Azur is divided into six sections to cover the six most important aspects of your visit to the region. It includes:

- The author's view of the area and its people
- Suggested walks and drives
- The Top 25 sights to visit
- The best of the rest – what to see while you're visiting
- Detailed listings of restaurants, hotels, shops and nightlife
- Practical information

In addition, easy-to-read side panels provide fascinating extra facts and snippets, highlights of places to visit and invaluable practical advice.

CROSS-REFERENCES

To help you make the most of your visit, cross-references, indicated by ➤, show you where to find additional information about a place or subject.

MAPS

The fold-out map in the wallet at the back of the book is a large-scale map of Provence and the Côte d'Azur.

The Top 25 locator maps found on the inside front and inside back covers of the book itself are for quick reference. They show the Top 25 sights, described on pages 24–48, which are clearly plotted by number (**1**–**25**, not page number) in alphabetical order.

PRICES

Where appropriate, an indication of the cost of an attraction is given by ✋ Expensive, Moderate or Inexpensive. An indication of the cost of a restaurant is given by € signs: €€€ denotes higher prices, €€ denotes average prices, while € denotes lower prices.

PROVENCE & THE CÔTE D'AZUR
life

A Personal View

It looked astonishingly beautiful in Maurice Pagnol's films *Jean de Florette* and *Manon des Source*, and Peter Mayle's celebrated books present life there as an idyll, but what is Provence really like?

Is it the untamed marshes of the Camargue; or the snow-clad mountains of the Alps; or perhaps the shimmering heat of the beautiful beaches and the exotic palms of the chic resorts which line the Mediterranean coastline?

Most visitors are at a loss to know where to start, such is the variety of the landscape and the wealth of ancient history. But for many, the true essence of Provence can be found in the myriad sleepy medieval villages, precariously perched on steep hillsides or hidden in a sun-drenched landscape of silvery olive groves, vineyards and parasol pines, splashed with poppy fields and scented stripes of lavender, stretching like mauve corduroy across the countryside, the air heavy with all the perfumes of Provence, and the countryside painted with the vivid palette of van Gogh and Cézanne.

No wonder Provence and the Côte d'Azur is France's most visited region, with its exceptional cultural heritage, and its wonderful rich diversity of landscape, cuisine, climate and peoples. Yet despite its popularity, it is still possible to escape the tourist hordes and discover your own hidden delights – tiny sun-kissed vineyards and secret sun-baked coves; bustling markets; romantic châteaux or a dusty game of boules; coffee and croissants in a village café, pastis in a bar…

The countryside is swathed in lavender on the Valensole Plain

Menton's sheltered bay, protected by a ring of mountains

The many facets and charms of Provence and the Côte d'Azur are impossible to chart, so varied are they, making choices almost impossible. Should you pack your paintbox, walking boots, swimsuit, skis or all of them? One suggestion is that on your first visit concentrate solely on the ambience – the brilliant sunshine, the sparkling air, the superb food, the unforgettable scenery and the friendly locals – for it is certain you will become a devotee and return again and again to experience what the addicted already know, but would rather keep to themselves!

New visitors soon fall under the region's spell. Those who already know it remain enchanted, returning year after year for a taste of *la vie Provençale*.

BOUNDARIES

The region of Provence and the Côte d'Azur is difficult to define as, since the Roman *Provincia* of 125BC, Provence's borders have moved countless times. Today it comprises the region Provence-Alpes-Côte-d'Azur, made up of the *départements* Alpes-Maritimes, Bouches-du-Rhône, Alpes-de-Haute-Provence, Hautes-Alpes, Var and Vaucluse. Officially, the Côte d'Azur stretches from the French-Italian frontier to St-Raphaël, although the expression is frequently applied to the whole French Riviera as far as Marseille.

Bringing in the grape harvest – Côtes du Rhône

Provence & the Côte d'Azur in Figures

GEOGRAPHY
- One of 22 regions of France
- *Départements*: Alpes-Maritimes, Alpes-de Haute-Provence, Bouches-du-Rhône, Hautes-Alpes, Vaucluse and Var
- Surface area: 31,436sq km (Monaco: 2sq km)
- Protected monuments and buildings: over 1,500
- Highest mountain: La Meije (3,983m)

PEOPLE
- Inhabitants: approximately 4.5 million (including about 375,000 foreigners); 90 per cent live in large cities and their suburbs
- Largest city: Marseille (population: 1.2 million)

CLIMATE
- Average annual temperature range: -1°C–22°C (mountains); 6°C–24°C (coast)
- Sea temperature range: 10°–25°C
- Annual hours of sunshine: 3,000 (over 300 days a year)
- Annual rainfall: 550–820mm (Nov and Mar are wettest)
- *Mistral* wind: up to 290kph; 100–150 days a year

AGRICULTURE & INDUSTRY
- Flowers produced: around 172 million roses and 188 million carnations annualy
- Percentage of national production: lavender oil (approximately 46 per cent)
- Classified wine regions: 10
- Vineyards: about 16 per cent of region's agricultural land

TOURISM
- Annual visitors to the area: around 3.6 million
- Tourist revenue: €10 billion per annum
- With nearly 10 million passengers in 2006, Nice's Côte d'Azur International airport has overtaken Marseille and Lyon as France's third busiest (after those in Paris)
- The area has 883km of coast; 135 marinas with 60,000 plus berths; 3 national parks and 4 regional natural parks; 100 classified museums; 60 ski/winter sports destinations; 66 golf courses

People of Provence & the Côte d'Azur

Ever since Dijonais vineyard owner Stephen Liegeard first visited the Mediterranean in 1887 and exclaimed 'Côte d'Azur!' (thereby christening an already popular winter health resort), a rich assortment of actors, artists, writers and royalty have been attracted to this southern coast of France, from Queen Victoria to Pablo Picasso, and from Frédéric Mistral to Peter Mayle, all seduced by the beauty of its landscapes and the sparkling azure sea. As Nietzche wrote in 1883: 'Here, the days follow on with a beauty that I would describe as almost insolent. I have never lived through a winter of such constant perfection.'

Star Quality
It was not until the 1930s that the Riviera became a summer resort, made fashionable by visiting Americans, including Harpo Marx, Isadora Duncan, who met her tragic death here when her scarf became entangled round the axle of her open car, and writer F Scott Fitzgerald. Nowadays, the Riviera remains home to Brigitte Bardot, Joan Collins, Elton John, Claudia Schiffer and a whole host of celebrities.

Inspirational Provence
Several writers have been drawn to Provence over the years and it has been the focus of countless literary masterpieces. However, it is the artists who have left the deepest imprint on the region – Renoir, Dufy, Matisse, Cézanne and van Gogh to name but a few.

They have immortalised Provence's most prestigious sites on canvas, having been hypnotised by the rich palette of landscapes and almost magical, incandescent light, which has provided inspiration over centuries – as it does today for a new generation of artists and writers.

WHO'S WHO
An A–Z of other local luminaries: Georges Bizet, Dirk Bogarde, Napoléon Bonaparte, Louis Bréa, Albert Camus, Winston Churchill, Jean Cocteau, Lawrence Durrell, Ernest Hemingway, Victor Hugo, Grace Kelly, D H Lawrence, Katherine Mansfield, Somerset Maugham, Nostradamus, Jean-Marie Le Pen, Marcel Pagnol, Francesco Petrarch, Robert Louis Stevenson, Patrick Süskind, Toulouse-Lautrec, Emile Zola.

A statue in Arles commemorating Frédéric Mistral, Provence's most famous poet

A Chronology

900,000 BC	First signs of human settlement.
c600 BC	Greeks found port of Massalia (Marseille).
300 BC	Celtic invasions of Provence.
218 BC	Hannibal crosses region to reach Italy.
125 BC	Romans conquer southern Gaul and name it Provincia.
58–52 BC	Caesar's conquest of Gaul.
3rd–5th Century AD	Spread of Christianity.
395	Arles becomes administrative capital of Roman Gaul.
476	Fall of Roman Empire.
536	Provence comes under Frankish rule.
8–10th Century	Saracens invade southern France; Provence becomes part of the Carolingian empire.
855	Kingdom of Provence created for Charlemagne's grandson, Charles the Bald.
1032	Provence becomes part of Holy Roman Empire.
1266	Charles I of Anjou, (already duke of Provence) is crowned King of Provence.
1308	The Genoese Grimaldi family purchases the estate of Monaco.
1309	Frenchman Clement V becomes Pope; Papacy established in Avignon until 1376.
1481	Death of Good King René. Region falls to France.
1501	Provençal parliament founded in Aix.
1559	Town and duchy of Orange fall to William of Nassau, Prince of Orange.

1691	Nice occupied by the French, but returned to Savoy in 1696.
1720	Plague kills over 100,000 people.
1789	French Revolution. Republicans adopt army song *La Marseillaise*.
1791	France annexes Avignon and the Comtat Venaissin.
1814	Napoléon lands in Provence.
1830s	Beginnings of tourism on the French Riviera.
1854	Foundation of the Félibrige literary circle with the aim of promoting the Provençal language.
1860	Nice votes to join France.
1866	Monte-Carlo founded; casino opened in 1878.
1920s–30s	Côte d'Azur becomes a fashionable resort.
1933	Waters of the Rhône first harnessed for energy.
1942	Nazis invade southern France.
1944	Allied troops land on the Côte d'Azur.
1956	Monaco's Prince Rainer III marries Grace Kelly.
1959	Floods in Fréjus kill 421.
1962	Algerian war of independence; many French North Africans settle in Provence.
1972	Regionalisation of French *départements*; five form the region Provence-Alpes-Côte-d'Azur.
1980s	Extreme-right political parties gain popularity in key Provençal cities.
1992	Floods devastate parts of the Vaucluse.
2007	60th anniversary of the Cannes Film Festival.

Best of Provence & the Côte d'Azur

Anyone for a game of boules?

If you only have a short time to visit Provence and the Cote d'Azur, or would like to get a really complete picture of the region, here are the essentials:

- Soak up the sun on one of the Riviera's sandy beaches, or relax under the shade of a classic striped parasol.

- Visit a perfumery in Grasse and create your very own Provençal scent (► 51).

- Taste some of the world's finest wines at Châteauneuf-du-Pape.

- Taste *la vraie bouillabaisse* in Marseille, near the old port where the dish originated.

- Spot the rich and famous at the Cannes Film Festival, the glitziest, most glamorous event of them all.

- Try your hand at gambling in Monte-Carlo's world-famous casino.

- Don your diamonds and the latest in haute couture and promenade the waterfront at St-Tropez, admiring its ostentatious yachts and gin palaces.

The colourful daily market in the heart of the old town of Grasse

- Splash through the marshes of the Camargue on horseback, accompanied by local *gardian* cowboys (► 30).

- Go shopping in a bright, bustling village market, and treat yourself to a relaxing picnic of goodies – goat's cheese, tomatoes, olives and wine – in the sleepy, surrounding countryside.

- Join locals in a game of boules – this ancient game originated here and, although it is now played all round the world, the most fiercely contested games still take place in the shady squares of Provence.

PROVENCE & THE CÔTE D'AZUR
how to organise your time

13

A Walk Around Arles

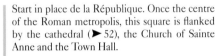

Start in place de la République. Once the centre of the Roman metropolis, this square is flanked by the cathedral (➤ 52), the Church of Sainte Anne and the Town Hall.

INFORMATION

Distance 2km
Time 1 hour/full day with visits
Start/end point place de la République

Lunch La Paillotte (€)
✉ 28 rue du Dr-Fanton (north of place du Forum)
☎ 04 90 96 33 15

Leave the square up rue du Cloître past the Théâtre Antique. Go right into rue de la Calade, anticlockwise around the Arène (➤ 52) past place de la Major, then right down rue Raspail. Sunny place de la Major, with its tiny Romanesque church, affords sweeping views across the Crau plain to the Alpilles hills and is scene of the famous *Fête des Gardians* on 1 May (➤ 22).

Cross rue 4-Septembre into rue de Grille towards the Rhône. Turn right along the river bank past Musée Rêattu (entrance in rue du Grand-Prieure) until you reach place Constantin.

Musée Réattu, housed in a 15th-century priory, contains an intriguing set of 57 coloured sketches by Picasso.

Turn left up rue Dominique-Maisto, past the Themes de Constantin and straight on into rue de l'Hôtel-de-Ville. Turn right at rue des Arènes until you reach place du Forum.

Place de la République in the ancient town of Arles

Place du Forum is the heart of Arles and a favourite meeting place for locals and tourists. Note the Corinthian columns embedded into the wall of the Hôtel Nord-Pinus (➤ 71).

Leave the square along rue du Palais and go right into rue Balze, past the Cryptoportiques. Bear left at rue Mistral, then left into the busy pedestrian shopping street, rue de la République, past Muséon Arlaten, which has an exhibition of costume, and back to place de la République.

A Walk Around St-Tropez

Start on the waterfront. Beside the Tourist Office, go through the Porte de la Poissonnerie, past the marble slabs of the daily fish market into place aux Herbes.

A stone's throw from the glamour of the quayside, the colourful daily fish, fruit and vegetable stalls remind visitors of St-Tropez' modest village past.

Leave the square up the steps of rue du Marché, turn left into rue des Commerçants, first right into rue du Clocher to Église St-Tropez. Before the church, turn left along rue Cdt-Guichard to place de la Mairie, dominated by its handsome pink and green town hall, and place Garrezio.

The massive tower here is all that remains of St-Tropez' oldest building, 10th-century Château de Suffren, once home of the great 18th-century seaman, Admiral Suffren.

Return past the town hall and along rue de la Ponche. The 15th-century Porche de la Ponche archways lead to the old Ponche quarter.

This is the old fishing district of St-Tropez, centred on the sun-baked place du Revelin, over-looking the unspoiled fishing port and tiny shingle beach.

Head up rue des Remparts, right at rue d'Aumale to the delightful place de l'Ormeau, and left up rue de l'Ormeau to rue de la Citadelle. Proceed downhill towards the port, taking the first left into rue Portail Neuf as far as the chapel.

The road alongside the Chapelle de la Miséricorde passes through its flying buttresses. The entrance to the chapel is on the rue Gambetta.

Go right down to rue Gambetta and turn left for lunch in place des Lices.

INFORMATION

Distance 1.5km
Time 1–1.5 hours, depending
   on church visits
Start end/point
   waterfront/place des
   Lices

Lunch Café des Arts (€)
   ✉ Place des Lices
   ☎ 04 94 97 02 25

Sandy coloured buildings overlook the harbour at St-Tropez

A Walk Around Nice Vielle Ville

Start at the western end of cours Saleya, where Nice's famous outdoor flower, fruit and vegetable market is held (► 44).

Go east past the palace of the former dukes of Savoy and the Italianate 18th-century Chapelle de la Misericorde to the yellow house at the end, where Matisse lived. Turn left into rue Gilly and continue along rue Droite, past Palais Lescaris.

INFORMATION

Distance 2km
Time 1–2 hours, depending on visits
Start/end point cours Saleya
🚌 All buses

Lunch Chez Freddy (€€)
✉ 22 cours Saleya
☎ 04 93 85 49 99

Rue Droite contains some of the old town's top galleries and Provence's best bread shops. Palais Lascaris, a 17th-century Genoese-style mansion, houses the Musée des Arts-et-Traditions-Populaires, containing sumptuous period paintings, furnishings and *trompe l'oeil* ceilings.

Continue straight on until place St-François and the early morning fish market.

Unusually, this is an inland fish market but, before the Paillon river was filled in, fishermen used to land here to sell their catch.

Return down rue St-Francois. Bear right into rue du Collet, left at place Centrale along rue Centrale, then right into rue Mascoïnat until you reach place Rossetti.

Place Rossetti is dominated by the baroque Cathédrale Ste-Réparate, with its emerald dome. Stop here for an ice cream at Fenocchio's (► 69).

A popular tourist spot, Nice's cours Saleya market

Leave the square along rue Ste-Réparate and then, at the end, turn right into rue de la Préfecture. The violinist Niccolò Paganini lived and died here at No 23.

A right turn opposite Paganini's house into rue St-Gaètan takes you back to cours Saleya.

A Walk Around Aix-en-Provence

This stroll takes you past some of Aix's finest fountains and mansions, while exploring the Quartier Mazarin and the old quarter.

Start at place Général de Gaulle and proceed up the right side of the café-filled cours Mirabeau. Opposite the Fontaine des 9 Canons, turn down rue Joseph Cabassol. A bit farther you will pass the Hotel de Caumont, built for the Marquis de Cabannes in the 18th century. At the end of rue Joseph Cabassol is the Lycée Mignet, once the Collège Bourbon.

Turn left down the Quatres Dauphins and look out for the 7th-century dolphin fountain. Continue on to the place St-Jean de Malte, where you will find the Église St-Jean-de-Malte and the Musée Granet. Take the next left and go left again back to the cours Mirabeau, acknowledging King René before crossing over to see the old advertisement for the Chapellerie du Cours Mirabeau at No 55, where Cézanne grew up in his father's hat shop.

Take the small passageway beside the shop, which leads to the place de Verdun, dominated by the 18th-century Palais de Justice. A regular flea market takes place here. Also worth a visit here is the Église Ste-Marie-Madeleine with works by Rubens and Louis-Michel Van Loo.

Carry on up rue Mignet, which has the crumbling façade of the ancient Monastère de la Visitation and several other fine 18th-century buildings. Take the next left down run Boulegon, and follow this through onto the place de l'Hôtel de Ville. From here you can return through the Vieil Aix backstreets to the cours Mirabeau for a much-deserved refreshment stop.

INFORMATION

Distance 2km
Time 2–3 hours
Start point place Général de Gaule
End point cours Mirabeau

Lunch Café les Deux-Garçons (€€)
✉ 53 cours Mirabeau
☎ 04 42 26 00 51

The 15th-century belfry visible high the above the Cathédrale St-Sauveur

17

A Drive from Arles Around Les Alpilles to Tarascon

INFORMATION

Distance 85km
Time 3 hours without stops;
full day with visits
Start end/point
Arles/Tarascon
✚ A2
Lunch Café des Arts, St-Rémy-
de-Provence
✉ 30 boulevard Victor-Hugo
☎ 04 90 92 08 50

Head northwest out of Arles along the N570, then the D17 to the Abbey of Montmajour. Once surrounded by marshes, this former Benedictine abbey is considered one of the most elaborate Romanesque churches in Provence.

Take the next turning right (D82), then over a crossroads, following signs to Aqueduc Romain. These two ruined aqueducts once conveyed water from the Alpilles to Arles.

Back at the crossroads, turn right past the old windmill that inspired 19th-century novelist Alphonse Daudet to write his masterwork *Lettres de mon Moulin* at Fontvieille. Leave town on the D17 through Paradou and continue to Maussane-les-Alpilles.

Taste the wines of the 14th-century Château d'Estoublon-Mogador just outside Fontvieille, or buy their prize-winning olive oil.

Once through Maussane, fork left on to the D78, following signs to le Destet and Eygalières (► 24). Exit Eygalières on the D74A. Turn left at the main road to St-Rémy-de-Provence (► 55). From here, take a small, unsignposted lane out of place de la République to St-Étienne-de-Grès.

St-Étienne is the home town of the Provençal fabric manufacturer Olivades. Visit their factory here.

Continue on the D32 towards Arles to reach a busy junction beside a church. The church is all that remains of the Gallo-Roman port of St-Gabriel, with one of the finest Romanesque façades in the Midi. The port flourished until the Middle Ages when the canal dried up.

Turn right at the junction, then take the D970 at the roundabout into Tarascon.

The Moulin de Daudet overlooking the Tarascon plain, near the town of Fontvieille

A Drive Around the Lubéron

Starting in Apt (▶ 37), take the D22 northeast towards Rustrel, then right at the crossroads to Bouvene.

The enormous old ochre quarries of Colorado de Rustrel are a colourful attraction – an almost lunar landscape of mounds, pillars, cliffs and hollows in every imaginable shade of ochre from pale yellow to blood red, set against deep pine forest. (From Bouvene it is a 50-minute walk.)

Back at the crossroads, continue on the D179 then the D943 to St-Saturnin-les-Apt. Leave the village on the D2 to Gordes (▶ 35). After Gordes, continue along the D2 towards Cavaillon, then take the first left (D103) signposted Apt and Beaumettes. Go straight on at the roundabout, following signs up to the centre of Ménerbes.

Outside Ménerbes, the Domaine de la Citadelle has a unique museum of corkscrews (Musée du Tire-Bouchon) dating back to the 17th century, along with complimentary wine tasting.

Leave Ménerbes on the D103, then the D109, past the Renaissance abbey of St-Hilaire to Lacoste. Lacoste vies with neighbouring villages Ménerbes, Bonnieux and Oppède-le-Vieux for the title of prettiest Lubéron village – a cinematic *village perché*, rich, exclusive and crowned by an 11th-century fortress, which in its heyday was one of the region's grandest.

Further along the D109 you reach Bonnieux (▶ 37). Leave the village on the D3, then first left (D149) to Pont Julien. This bridge is reputedly the best-preserved Roman bridge in France.

Turn right at the main road (N100) for the return journey to Apt.

INFORMATION

Distance 90km
Time 2.5 hours without stops;
full day with visits
Start/end point Apt
🚩 B2
Lunch Le Fournil, Bonnieux
✉ 5 place Camot
☎ 04 90 75 83 62

Stepped, terraced buildings cling to the hillside, Gordes

Finding Peace & Quiet

Nature has been infinitely generous with Provence and the Côte d'Azur. You only need to wander through the fields and forests, to hike in the hills, gorges and mountains or to stroll along the shore to discover a vast array of flora and fauna in these varied habitats. It is, without doubt, a naturalist's paradise.

THE COAST

With the colourful bird life of the Riviera, in particular the bright yellow serins and Sardinian warblers of the rocky Esterel coast, it is easy to forget that hidden out of sight the Mediterranean supports an abundance of marine creatures. Port-Cros, one of the Îles d'Hyères, and France's only offshore national park, provides a rare opportunity to see the region's rich underwater life. Armed with a mask and flippers, and following a unique underwater path, it is possible to swim with vividly coloured fish (sea peacocks, black-faced blennies), while octopuses and jellyfish lurk among beds of Neptune grass, sponges and sea anemones.

Provence's best-known wildlife location and one of Europe's most important wetlands is the Camargue, famous for its white horses, black bulls, pink flamingos and some of Europe's most exotic birds.

A flamingo preening its feathers within the Parc Ornithologique du Pont de Gau

THE HINTERLAND

In the _arrière pays_, northwest of the Camargue, lies the rarely visited plaine de la Crau, a stony plain with sun-bleached scrub and the occasional rock pool, an ideal habitat for both insects and reptiles. Indeed, five species of non-poisonous snake can be found here. Look out also for pin-tailed sandgrouse, cream-bibbed pratincole and the dazzling orange, yellow, green, blue and black bee-eater, one of Provence's most colourful birds, which feeds on bees and dragonflies caught on the wing. The low, craggy limestone Alpilles massif beyond attracts birds of prey, including Bonelli's eagle, Egyptian vultures and eagle owls.

Beautiful butterflies enhance the Parc National du Mercantour

One of Provence's special delights is to ramble through the region's extensive brushwood habitats (locally called *garrigue*), where the air is fragrant with lavender and the wild herbs – rosemary, thyme, basil, marjoram and tarragon, the delicious *herbes de Provence* – so prominent in regional cuisine.

While its *garrigue* vegetation harbours warblers, hoopoes and blue rock thrushes, the region's sunshine and favourable climate allow many interesting trees to grow, with olive and oak predominant in lower areas, pines, almonds and neat rows of cypresses on the hillsides of the interior, and an abundance of fruit trees. After all, Provence is the market garden of France.

Warm sunshine ripens the olives near Nyons, the principal area for this Provençal crop

THE MOUNTAINS

Up in the Hautes-Alpes, the Parc Régional de Queyras is a wild, forgotten corner of the Alps bordering Italy, renowned for its rare wild flowers.

To the south, one of France's most beautiful alpine reserves – the Parc National du Mercantour – provides sanctuary for most of Europe's mountain animal species, including wild boar, marmot, chamois, ibex and mouflon (wild sheep), as well as bright butterflies. The sweet, heady perfume of myriad alpine flowers attracts a busy insect life of beetles, bugs and bees – an endless supply of food for the 18 types of bat common to the area.

The steep, scrub-covered slopes of the Gorges du Verdon

21

What's On

JANUARY	Monte-Carlo Rally
FEBRUARY	Nice Carnival *Fête du Citron*, Menton *Corso du Mimosa*, Bormes-les-Mimosas, 17 Feb
APRIL	International Tennis Open, Monte-Carlo Wine-growers' Festival, Châteauneuf-du-Pape, 25 Apr Easter Festival and start of bullfighting season, Arles, 4 days at Easter
MAY	*Fête des Gardians*, Arles Cannes Film Festival *Bravade de St-Torpes*, St-Tropez, 16–17 May International Formula One Grand Prix, Monaco *Ochre Festival*, Roussillon (Ascension weekend) Gypsy Pilgrimage, Stes-Maries-de-la-Mer, 24–25 May
JUNE	Jazz Festival, Aix *Fête de la Tarasque*, Tarascon
JULY	Nice Jazz Festival (first 2 weeks) International Folklore Festival, Marseille (first 2 weeks) *Rencontres Internationales de la Photographie*, Arles Annual Provençal Boules Competition, Marseille (mid-Jul) *Chorègies Music Festival*, Orange (last 2 weeks) International Art Festival, Cagnes International Theatre Festival, Avignon (mid-Jul to mid-Aug)
JULY/AUGUST	Over 300 towns and villages have summer festi- vals (listings available from regional tourist offices)
AUGUST	Grape-ripening Festival, Châteauneuf-du-Pape Lavender Festival, Sault *Fête de St-Laurent*, Eygalières, 9–11 Aug
SEPTEMBER	Rice Harvest Festival and end of bullfighting season, Arles (2nd Sun)
NOVEMBER	Santon Fair, Marseille (last Sun–Epiphany)

PROVENCE &
THE CÔTE D'AZUR
top 25 sights

The sights are shown on the maps on the inside front cover and inside back cover, numbered **1**–**25** alphabetically

Les Alpilles

INFORMATION

➕ A2

ℹ️ Les Baux-de-Provence
Tourist Office: Maison du
Roy (☎ 04 90 54 34 39;
www.lesbauxdeprovence.
com)

↔️ Arles (► 26), St-Rémy-
de-Provence (► 55)

**Les-Baux-de-Provence
Citadelle**

✉️ Ville Morte

☎ 04 90 54 55 56;
www.chateau-baux-
provence.com

🕐 Mar–Oct daily 9–6.30
(Jul–Aug until 9); Dec–Jan
9–5; Nov, Feb 9–5

💰 Moderate

South of St-Rémy-de-Provence lies a dramatic and arid landscape of crumpled white limestone crags, the Chaîne des Alpilles.

Market gardens, vineyards and long avenues of plane trees on the lower slopes give way to olive groves, and scrub splashed with yellow broom, lilac lavender and scented wild thyme. This area is easy to explore on foot, horseback or bike, and you are unlikely to meet anyone except the occasional flock of sheep.

Often called 'Pompeii of Provence', the ancient ruined citadel of les Baux-de-Provence clings to one of the highest ridges of the Alpilles. Lex Baux is divided into two: the bustling inhabited lower village, where elegant Renaissance houses line the shiny cobbled streets, and the deserted Ville Morte perched above, its ruined buildings hardly distinguishable from the surrounding limestone crags.

During the Middle Ages, this was the seat of the seigneurs de Baux, one of southern France's most powerful families. Their Cour d'Amour – a dazzling society of lords, ladies and wandering troubadours – was renowned throughout the Midi and, ever since, les Baux has been a romantic pilgrimage centre for poets and painters.

The picturesque village of Eygalières is hidden off the beaten track, surrounded by a wild, dusty landscape of olive and cypress trees. Its creamy stone houses, with sky blue and aquamarine shutters, line the lanes leading up to the village chapel, a ruined castle and a spectacular panorama of the Alpilles. A good time to visit is during the first weekend of August, when this sleepy village hosts a merry fête and a splendid torchlit *Arlésienne* horseback parade.

Les-Baux-de-Provence (above), on a rocky spur projecting from the Alpilles chain. Walking the white limestone paths (top) is a highlight of a visit here

Aix-en-Provence

The old capital of Provence is splashed by over 100 fountains, a reminder that it was named after its waters, Aquae Sextiae, by the Romans in 123BC.

The city thrived culturally during the Middle Ages under Good King René, an ardent patron of the arts, reaching the height of its splendour during the 17th and 18th centuries, with the construction of over 160 honey-hued *hôtels* particuliers (mansion residences), beautifully decorated with ornamental wrought-iron balconies.

Paul Cézanne, Aix's most famous citizen, spent much of his life here, painting the rugged limestone hills of the surrounding countryside. A special circuit *Cézanne* around town, marked by bronze pavement plaques, leads to the studio where he spent the last seven years of his life – poignantly just as he left it, with unfinished canvases, palettes and his old black hat.

Cours Mirabeau, a mansion-lined avenue framed by a canopy of plane trees, plays centre stage to the wealthy Aixois society who promenade their poodles here between cups of coffee in Les Deux Garçons (➤ 64) and other Parisian-style cafés. The *cours* divides the town centre: the *vieille ville* (old town) to the north, and the Quartier Mazarin, with its fancy mansions, to the south. Other highlights include the Cathédrale St-Sauveur (➤ 52) and the Musée Granet (➤ 50).

INFORMATION

➕ B2
🏠 2 place du Général-de-Gaulle (☎ 04 42 16 11 61; www.aixenprovence.com)
↔ The Lubéron (➤ 37), Marseille (➤ 38)

Detail of carving (above) on a solid walnut door on St-Sauveur cathedral

Aix-en-Provence is a city of fountains (left)

Arles

INFORMATION

🔲 A2

ℹ️ Boulevard des Lices
(☎ 04 90 18 41 20;
www.arlestourisme.com)

Église St-Trophime

✉️ Place de la République

☎️ 04 90 96 07 38

🕐 May–Sep daily 9–6.30;
Oct, Mar–Apr 9–6;
Nov–Feb 10–5

♿ Few

🎫 Cloister: moderate

After centuries of fame as the Roman capital of Provence, then as a medieval ecclesiastical centre, Arles seemed content to live on its former glory.

Recently, however, it has become a lively city, largely due to several new cultural events, including an internationally renowned photographic fair, a rekindled French passion for bullfighting and the influence of local fashion designer, Christian Lacroix (► 75), whose creations reflect the colourful traditional Arlesian costumes.

For centuries, Arles has attracted artists and writers. The beautiful women of the city inspired Daudet's story *L'Arlésienne*, Bizet's opera of the same name and the *farandole*, a medieval dance. Picasso visited to paint the bullfights, and van Gogh moved here in 1888 and lived with Gauguin in the famous yellow house (destroyed in the war), which he immortalised on canvas (*La Maison Jaune*) along with other pictures of Arles including *Café de Nuit*.

The Église St-Trophime is a masterpiece of Provençal Romanesque. The original church was built in the 5th century, then rebuilt at the end of the 11th century, and the ornate tympanum, depicting the Last Judgement, was added in the next century. By contrast, the austerity of the interior is striking. The cloister of St-Trophime, with rich carvings and illuminated chapels hung with Aubusson tapestries, is among the treasures of Provence. Arles' other glorious landmarks include the Roman amphitheatre and necropolis of Les Alyscamps (► 52).

Not only is Arles a city of the arts and an ancient and cultural crossroads, but it is also surrounded by beautiful countryside, making it an ideal centre for exploring the jagged Alpille mountains (► 24), the fertile banks of the Rhône (► 32) and the untamed Camargue (► 30).

People gather in the place du Forum (top). The shady alleyways of Arles (above)

Avignon

The city of Avignon – administrative centre of the Vaucluse and a major artistic area – is an important city in the history of France.

Strategically located near the junction of the Rhône and Durance rivers, it has been the scene of countless conflicts since Roman times, and for over a century it was the seat of the popes and centre of a religious and political power struggle. It was a French pope, Clement V, who first moved his residence from the Vatican to Avignon in 1309. From then on, a succession of French popes and cardinals built up a powerful base here, constructing a cornucopia of architectural treasures within the city's massive fortifications to display their wealth; the most impressive of these being the Palais des Papes (➤ 52–53). Following pressure from the rest of Europe, the papal establishment transferred back to Rome in 1377. However, a group of French cardinals refused to accept this and elected a series of rival antipopes who, over the next 40 years, continued to exercise authority from Avignon, creating what is today known as the Great Schism.

A walk along the ramparts reveals the two sides of Avignon today – the village-like atmosphere of the historic walled town, its skyline adorned with steeples and monuments, and the sprawling factories and suburbs beyond. It is a cheerful, lively place, especially in July when the narrow lanes and pedestrian zones resound with buskers, street theatre and café cabarets during the renowned theatre festival. If you are interested in art, the Musée du Petit Palais (➤ 51), Musée Calvet (➤ 51) and the Musée Angladon (➤ 50) are worth a look, and the Palais du Roure (➤ 51) houses a museum of Provençal history. But Avignon's biggest draw is its famous bridge, Pont St-Bénézet (➤ 53), immortalised in the song *Sur le pont d'Avignon*.

INFORMATION

🔲 A1
🔲 41 cours Jean-Jaurés
(☎ 04 32 74 32 74;
www.ot-avignon.fr)
🔲 Orange (➤ 55)

Sur le pont d'Avignon
*(top). A statue
surmounting the tower
of the Chapelle
Clementine (above),
Palais des Papes*

27

Biot

The charming hilltop village is a mass of steep cobbled lanes, lined with quaint sand-coloured houses capped by orange-tiled roofs.

At the heart of the village is the famous arcaded main square, place des Arcades. At the south end is the tiny place l'Église, where a doorway in a crumbling bell tower leads into a surprisingly capacious church hidden behind the houses. Most of the delightful streets radiating out from the square are decorated with huge earthenware jars ablaze with geraniums and tropical plants. For centuries, Biot has been a thriving pottery centre. It is also known for its gold and silverwork, ceramics, olive-wood carving and glassworks. Visitors can watch glass-blowers at the Verrerie de Biot demonstrating their unique *verre bullé* (bubble glass).

Near by, the striking Musée Fernand-Léger, with its huge brilliantly coloured mosaic façade and monumental stained-glass windows, was founded in 1959 in memory of cubist painter Fernand Léger, who lived at Biot for a short time and inspired the growth of the craft workshops here. The museum contains nearly 400 of his works, including ceramics, tapestries, stained glass and mosaics.

INFORMATION

- ✚ D2
- 🛈 46 rue St-Sébastien
  (☎ 04 93 65 78 00;
  www.biot.fr)
- ↔ Cagnes-sur-Mer ➤ (56),
  Cannes (➤ 56), Nice
  (➤ 44), St-Paul-de-Vence
  (➤ 55)

Musée Fernand-Léger

- ✉ Chemin du Val de Pome
- ☎ 04 92 91 50 30;
  www.musee-
  fernandleger.fr
- 🕐 Jul–Sep Wed–Mon
  10.30–6; Oct–Jun
  10–12.30, 2–5.30. Closed
  25 Dec, 1 Jan, 1 May
- ♿ Good
- 💷 Moderate
- ❓ Phone in advance to
  arrange guided tours

Glass for sale in the gardens of Verrerie de Biot (above). Church towers surmount the tight cluster of hilltop buildings that form the village of Biot (right)

The Calanques

The most dramatic scenery of the French Riviera – dazzling white cliffs plunging into the sparkling turquoise waters of magnificent mini-fjords.

INFORMATION

➕ B3
♿ None
💲 Free
🚌 Cassis (► 56), Marseille (► 38)
❓ Various boat trips leave from Cassis harbour; arrive early and look for boats that are loading passengers

This fjord-like landscape is unique in Europe. Just outside Cassis, the coast is broken up by a series of tiny, narrow creeks or *calanques*, lying at the foot of sheer limestone cliffs. The vertical, weathered rock faces are popular with climbers and the clear, deep water is ideal for bathing, making the area a popular weekend retreat from nearby Marseille.

The Calanques can only be reached by pleasure cruiser from Cassis or on foot, following a waymarked path across the heather and gorse of the high clifftops, with a steep scramble down to the beaches. The first and longest *calanque*, Port-Miou, is one of the most picturesque, lined with yachts and pleasure craft. Calanque Port-Pin is the smallest, with a tiny shingle beach shaded by pines (hence the name, although many trees here were destroyed some years ago by a massive forest fire). En Vau, the third inlet, is the most spectacular, with stark precipitous cliffs and needle-like rocks rising from the sea. The 90-minute walk to reach it, and the ensuing steep descent to the sandy beach keep it free from crowds.

Further west, the Sormiou and Morgiou creeks can be reached by car. In 1991, French diver Henri Cosquer discovered a Stone Age grotto deep below sea level at Sormiou. It is decorated with ancient paintings of prehistoric animals, similar to those found at Lascaux in the Dordogne. There are doubts about the paintings' authenticity, but, unfortunately, no palaeolithic experts have the ability to dive to 32m in order to decide whether they are genuine.

The deeply indented limestone shoreline of Les Calanques (above). Rivers winding through the landscape make for a boating hotspot (below)

The Camargue

INFORMATION

✚ A2

A disparate marshland, renowned for its passionate people, its traditions, its silver-cream horses, black bulls and salmon-pink flamingos.

No area in France matches the Camargue for its landscape: brackish lagoons, flat rice fields and salty marshes, sand spits and coastal dunes, tufted with coarse, spiky grass and interlaced with shallow streams and canals. Even its boundaries – the lesser and greater Rhône deltas and the sea – are forever shifting. This extraordinary landscape harbours an outstanding variety of wildlife and the unique lifestyle of the Camarguais cowboys.

The people of the Camargue are hardy folk. They live in low, thatched, whitewashed cottages with bulls' horns over the door to ward off evil spirits. They proudly guard the Camarguais heritage by wearing traditional costume and raising horses and cattle on ranches, or *manades*. Contrary to popular belief the famous white horses are not wild. They are actually owned by a *manadier* or breeder, but are left to roam semi-free. Some are also used for trekking expeditions. The small, black local bulls, with their distinctive lyre-shaped horns, are bred for the ring. Watching a mounted *gardian* drive his herd through the marshes is a truly unforgettable sight!

The Camargue also offers sanctuary to some of Europe's most exotic water birds, including purple herons and stone curlews. It is the only place in Europe where flamingos breed regularly and in their greatest numbers between April and September. The best months for birdwatching are from April to June and then from September to February.

Flamingos (above) and a glossy ibis (below), two of the many species of birdlife of the Camargue

The Corniches

Cutting through the mountains at different levels and edging the golden coast, the corniches offer stunning views of the azure sea.

Three famous corniches (cliff roads) traverse the most scenic and most mountainous stretch of the Côte d'Azur from Nice to Menton via Monaco. Called La Grande (D2564), La Moyenne (N7) and L'Inférieure, they each zig-zag their way along vertiginous ledges at three different elevations. La Grande Corniche, at the highest level, was first constructed by Napoléon and is by far the best choice for picnickers and lovers of plants and wildlife.

The lowest route (Corniche Inférieure) follows the coastal contours through all the seaside resorts, and is best avoided in the main tourist season of July and August.

The steep Corniche Moyenne in the middle is undoubtedly the most dramatic – a cliff-hanging route with hair-raising bends, sudden tunnels and astounding views, frequently used for car commercials and movie car chases.

INFORMATION

➕ D2
🔁 Nice (➤ 44), Monaco (➤ 39), Èze (➤ 33)

Viewed from the road, boats at anchor in the bay of Villefranche-sur-Mer (top).
A picture-postcard view of the Riviera coast from the steep terraces of Eze (below)

Côtes du Rhône

INFORMATION

Beaumes-de-Venise
- A1
- Place du Marché (☎ 04 90 62 94 39; www. otbeaumesdevenise.com)

Châteauneuf-du-Pape
- A1
- Place du Portail (☎ 04 90 83 71 08)
- Orange (➤ 55)
- Wine festival: first weekend in Aug

Gigondas
- A1
- Place du Portail (☎ 04 90 65 85 46; www.gigondas-dm.fr)

An ancient château (top) overlooking the wine-producing village of Gigondas. Wide stretches of vineyards in the Côtes du Rhône (below), noted for the production of robust, full-bodied wines

The stony, sun-baked, red-clay soil of the southern Rhône nurtures France's most prestigious wines – fine and full-bodied with a spicy bouquet.

Numerous wine routes lead you through charming, yellow-stone villages with shady squares, old fountains and red-tiled roofs, hidden in a sea of vineyards and largely given over to restaurants and cellars offering free wine tasting.

The village of Beaumes-de-Venise is majestically framed by the lacy silver crags of the Dentelles de Montmirail and is well known for its sweet golden, Muscat wines. Taste them at the Cave des Vignerons or during the region's annual wine festivals, accompanied by goat's cheese, foie gras and melons drowned in Muscat.

The wines of Châteauneuf-du-Pape are world-renowned as well, largely thanks to 13th-century Pope Jean XXII of Avignon. It was he who built the now-ruined château, with its splendid views, as a summer residence and planted the first vineyards. Many Côtes du Rhône wines are made from just one grape variety, but vintners here blend up to 13 different grapes to produce their distinctive wines of unique complexity. The Musée du Vin is dedicated to the history of local viticulture, and visitors can indulge in wine tastings.

Gigondas is a small, unspoiled village, set against the jagged backdrop of the Dentelles. Its wines are reputed to be the best in the area, notably the intense red Grenache.

Séguret, a charming, circular hilltop village has its own *appellation d'origine contrôlée*. The ochre cottages, with their turquoise shutters hidden behind vines and creeper, house craftspeople renowned for their dried flowers and *santons* (terracotta Christmas crib figurines).

Èze

Without doubt one of the Riviera's most impressive perched villages, Èze affords truly stunning views that will take your breath away.

Èze, the most strikingly situated and best-preserved Provençal *village perché*, stands high on a rocky pinnacle ten minutes' drive from Nice and Monaco. Frequently called the *Nid d'Aigle* (Eagle's Nest), it boasts spectacular views over the entire Riviera as far as Corsica.

Tall, golden stone houses and a labyrinth of tiny vaulted passages and stairways climb steeply up to the ruins of the once-massive Saracen fortress, 429m above sea level, surrounded by an exotic garden, bristling with magnificent cacti, succulents and rare palms. Take time to explore the countless craft shops housed in small caves within the rock – tiny treasure troves of antiques, ceramics, pewter and olive-wood carvings. At the foot of the hill, the two perfume factories of Galimard and Fragonard both offer a free guided tour.

INFORMATION

🗺 D2
🚏 Place de Gaulle
(☎ 04 93 41 26 00;
www.eze-riviera.com)
🔁 Cap-Ferrat (► 57), The
Corniches (► 31),
Menton (► 57), Monaco
(► 39), Nice (► 44)

Jardin Exotique d'Èze
✉ Rue du Château
☎ 04 93 41 10 30
🕐 Daily 9–6/7 (Jul, Aug
until 10)
♿ None
🎫 Moderate

Galimard Museum
✉ Place Géneral de Gaulle
☎ 04 93 41 10 70;
www.galimard.com
🕐 Daily 8.30–6.30
🎫 Free

Fragonard Factory
✉ Èze village, Moyenne
Corniche
☎ 04 93 41 05 05;
www.fragonard.com
🕐 Daily 8.30–6.30; closed
noon–2 Nov–Jan
🎫 Free

*Èze village (above)
standing proud on the
hillside. Take time to
explore the magical
narrow lanes (left)*

33

Fondation Maeght, St-Paul-de-Vence

- D2
- St-Paul-de-Vence
- 04 93 32 81 63; www.fondation-maeght.com
- Oct–Jun 10–12.30, 2.30–6; Jul–Sep 10–7
- Café
- Few
- Expensive
- St-Paul-de-Vence (➤ 55), Cagnes-sur-Mer (➤ 56)
- Cinema, gift shop and art library

A colourful mobile (top) displayed in the grounds of the Fondation. The galleries comprise entirely 20th-century art (above)

'A world in which modern art can both find its place and that other worldliness which used to be called supernatural.'

These words were spoken by André Malraux, minister of cultural affairs, during the opening of Fondation Maeght in 1964, a beautiful gallery which has since become one of the most distinguished modern-art museums in the world. It was the brainchild of Aimé and Marguerite Maeght, who were art dealers and close friends of Matisse, Miró, Braque, Bonnard and Chagall, and it was their private collection that formed the basis of the museum. The aim was to create an ideal environment in which to display contemporary art.

The small artful gallery that resulted is hidden amid umbrella pines above the quaint hilltop village of St-Paul-de-Vence. It is surrounded by a small park, which contains a collection of sculptures, mosaics and murals. The building itself blends into its natural surroundings, with massive windows, light traps in the roof, and extraordinary white cylindrical 'sails' atop the building. These are not solely decorative, but serve the dual purpose of collecting rainwater to work the fountains.

The Fondation Maeght's remarkable permanent collection includes works by nearly every major artist of the past 50 years. These are shown in rotation throughout the year, except during summer when temporary exhibitions are held. The star sights include the Cour Giacometti – a tiled courtyard peopled with skinny Giacometti figures – Chagall's vast, joyful canvas *La Vie*, Miró's *Labyrinthe*, and a fantastic multi-level maze of fountains, trees, mosaics and sculptures. There is also a chapel in the grounds, which contains stained glass by Braque, Ubec and Marq. It was built in memory of the Maeghts' son who died in 1953 at the age of 11.

Gordes & the Abbaye de Sénanque

Famous for its artists' colony, Cistercian abbey and ancient *borie* village, Gordes is a centre for touring the Lubéron.

Gordes is justifiably rated one of the most beautiful villages in France. Its grandiose church and Renaissance château rise from a golden plinth on a spur of Mont Ventoux, surrounded by narrow cobbled streets and tiers of golden sandstone houses that spill down the steep, stony slopes. During World War II, many buildings were ruined or abandoned and the village fell into decline until the 1960s, when cubist André l'Hote, constructivist Victor Vasarély and other artists brought new life to the village, restoring the delightful Renaissance houses and setting up attractive galleries, studios and boutiques. The castle currently contains the Museum of Pol Mara, a Flemish contemporary artist and honorary citizen of Gordes.

Just southwest of Gordes, the most famous collection of *bories* in France lies hidden in dusty scrubland. These extraordinary beehive-shaped, dry-stone huts sheltered the earliest farmers and semi-nomadic shepherds as early as the 3rd century BC. This particular village at Moulin des Bouillons was inhabited as recently as the last century, and is the largest and most complete of its kind in the world.

In a secluded valley north of Gordes, bathed in a sea of lavender, is one of the great symbols of Provence, the Cistercian abbey of Sénanque – one of France's best remaining examples of 12th-century religious architecture. The monks still follow a secret medieval recipe to concoct a pungent, herb-flavoured, yellow liqueur called Sénancole.

INFORMATION

🔳 B1
ℹ️ Le Château (☎ 04 90 72 02 75; www.gordes-vilage.com)
🔄 Fontaine-de-Vaucluse (➤ 54), Roussillon (➤ 45), The Lubéron (➤ 37)

Museum of Pol Mara
☎ 04 90 72 02 75
🕐 Daily 10–noon, 2–6; closed 25 Dec, 1 Jan
♿ Moderate

Village des Bories
✉️ D2 from Gordes
☎ 04 90 72 03 48
🕐 Daily 9–sunset
♿ Few
♿ Moderate

Abbaye de Sénanque
☎ 04 90 72 05 72; www.senanque.fr
🕐 Guided tours Feb to mid-Nov daily except Sun am; mid-Nov to Jan pm only

Abbaye de Sénanque rising out from the beautiful village of Gordes

Gorges du Verdon

INFORMATION

➕ C2

🏨 Hôtel de Ville, Aiguines
(☎ 04 94 70 21 64;
www.aiguines.com)

🔁 Moustiers-Ste-Marie
(► 55)

❓ Useful contacts: Les
Guides (☎ 04 94 07
46 96) for walkers and
climbers; Chanteraine
(☎ 04 94 70 22 60) for
horse riding; Aqua Viva
Est (☎ 04 92 83 75 74)
for canoeing, rafting and
mountain biking; Verdon
Passion (☎ 04 92 74 69
77) for hang-gliding and
biplanes

The deepest, longest, wildest canyon in Europe is like a dream come true for canoeists, climbers, white-water rafters and other sports lovers.

Over the centuries, the Verdon river, a tributary of the mighty Durance, has scored a magnificent gorge in the limestone plateau of the Alpes-de-Haute-Provence, stretching a staggering 21km from the Pont de Soleils down to the vast man-made lake of Ste-Croix. In places it is over 800m deep, the second deepest gorge in the world after the Grand Canyon and one of the great natural wonders of Provence. It was first explored as late as 1905 by Isadore Blanc. Before that, people were deterred by local stories of devils and 'wild men'.

The canyon is best approached from Castellane to the east. The bed of the canyon is impassable, and the river is only negotiable by trained sportsmen or with an official guide. Spectacular winding roads hairpin along the clifftops on both sides of the gorge, with frequent belvederes to park the car and peer giddily down to the green waters of the Verdon.

Drivers face a difficult decision whether to follow the northern Route des Crêtes, with its many magnificent viewpoints, or the southern Corniche Sublime, through the ancient hilltop villages of Trigance and Aiguines. Hardened walkers usually opt for the latter, leaving the road at the Pont Sublime for an awesome eight-hour trek down into the gorge, through dingy tunnels and along a series of narrow ledges above the river. Both car trails take approximately half a day, ending at Moustiers-Ste-Marie (► 55).

Goats at home on the mountainside

The Lubéron

Cedar and pine interspersed with lavender, herbs, vineyards and almond and olive groves, draped across a range of small mountains.

The dramatic wooded gorge of the Combe de Lourmarin (road D943) splits the region in two. The high, wild Grand Lubéron mountains lie to the east. Walkers tackling the strenuous climb from Auribeau to the uppermost peak of Mourre Nègre (1,100m) will be rewarded with views from the Basse-Alpes to the Mediterranean. To the west, the pretty *villages perchés* of the Petit Lubéron have long been one of France's most fashionable *residences secondaires*, even before Peter Mayle's bestseller, *A Year in Provence*.

Apt is a busy old market town north of the Lubéron mountains and is an ideal centre for touring the area. The best place to start is at the Maison du Parc Naturel Régional du Lubéron, which details walks and other outdoor activities, together with a small museum documenting local natural history.

At Lourmarin, an imposing château, the medieval houses made from local yellow stone and dressed in honeysuckle, tiny fountain-filled squares and a host of inviting restaurants create a beautiful ensemble on the southern slopes of the Lubéron.

The terracotta-roofed houses of Bonnieux wind up to a tiny, 12th-century chapel surrounded by sentinel-like cypresses. The village is spread out on a north-facing spur of the Petit Lubéron overlooking the vineyards, cherry trees and lavender fields of the Coulon valley, and its belvedere commands entrancing views over the Plateau de Vaucluse to mighty Mont Ventoux beyond. Once papal property, Bonnieux has preserved many fine monuments, including the Town Hall, a bakery museum and notable Renaissance paintings in its churches.

INFORMATION

➕ B2
Parc Naturel Régional du Lubéron
📍 Maison du Parc, place Jean-Jaurès, Apt (☎ 04 90 04 42 00; www.parcduluberon.com)
🕐 Mon–Fri 8.30–12, 1.30–6 (also Sat Apr–Sep)

Apt
➕ B2
ℹ️ 20 avenue Phillippe-de-Girard (☎ 04 90 74 03 18; www.ot-apt.fr)

Lourmarin
➕ B2
ℹ️ 9 avenue Phillippe-de-Girard (☎ 04 90 68 10 77)

Bonnieux
➕ B2
ℹ️ 7 place Carnot (☎ 04 90 75 91 90)

Bonnieux (above), rising towards the ancient ramparts. The streets of Apt (below)

Marseille

The amazing mix of race and culture in France's premier port and oldest city led Alexandre Dumas to describe Marseille as the 'meeting place of the entire world'.

INFORMATION

🔳 B3

ℹ️ 4 La Canebière
(☎ 04 91 13 89 00;
www.marseille-
tourisme.com)

🚇 Metro 1: Vieux Port

↔️ Aix–en–Provence (► 25),
Cassis (► 56)

**Basilique Notre-Dame
de-la-Garde**

✉️ Place Colonel Eden

☎ 04 91 13 40 80; www.
notredamedelagarde.com

🕐 Oct–May 7–7.15; Jun–Sep
7.15–8

🔲 60

♿ Good

🎟️ Free

*The old port (top).
Basilique Notre-Dame-
de-la-Garde (above)*

The city has a strong personality, its reputation sustained by political corruption, sporadic gangsterism and racial tension exacerbated by the National Front. It is also a traditional city, famous for its shipping, its soap, its pastis and the world's largest annual boules competition, and a city of contradictions and contrasts, from the seedy, congested downtown districts and the hideous high-rise suburbs to the vibrant old port, the sandy beaches and chic residences of the Corniche.

The main thoroughfare of Marseille, La Canebière, took its name from the Provençal *canébe* (cannabis), originally running from former hemp fields to the rope-making heart of the old port. Once considered the Champs Élysées of Marseille, lined with fancy shops, grand cafés and luxury hotels, it has since lost much of its former grandeur, but remains very much the place for shopping.

The Basilique Notre-Dame-de-la-Garde is Marseille's major landmark, standing proudly above the city, a massive neo-Byzantine extravaganza topped by a gaudy golden Madonna. Palais Longchamp, a grandiose 1860s palace, houses Marseille's main art gallery (closed for restoration), packed with masterpieces by Rubens, Brueghel, Corot and local Marseille artists.

Find time to see some of the many architectural gems, such as the recently discovered Roman Jardin des Vestiges, 5th-century Basilique St-Victor and ostentatious Cathédrale de la Major (1893), the largest to be built in France for many centuries.

Monaco

After the Vatican, Monaco is the world's smallest sovereign state, a 195-hectare, spotlessly clean strip of skyscraper-covered land squeezed between sea and mountains.

Monaco is the name of the principality and also the district on the peninsula to the south, containing the old town with its narrow streets and pastel-coloured houses, a startling contrast to the newer high-rise district of Monte-Carlo, centred round its glitzy casino and designer shops. With so much evident wealth and glamour, it is hard to imagine Monaco's turbulent past, at various times occupied by the French, the Spanish and the dukes of Savoy. The present ruling king is Prince Albert II, whose family, the Grimaldis, have ruled Monaco for over 700 years – the world's oldest reigning monarchy. When the royal family are not at home, guided tours are available of the Palais du Prince (▶ 53).

The Grimaldis once held sway over an area that extended along the coast and included Menton. However, their high taxes provoked a revolt and the principality shrank to its present size. Facing a financial crisis, Charles III of Monaco decided to turn to gambling for revenue by opening a casino. Such was its success that taxes were soon abolished altogether.

Even if you are not a gambler, it is worth visiting the world's most famous casino, designed in 1878 by Charles Garnier, architect of the Paris Opéra, to see the opulent belle-époque interior and tiny, highly ornate opera house, the Salle Garnier, which has been graced by many of the world's most distinguished opera singers. The dazzlingly illuminated place du Casino by night is a must see, and the Café de Paris and Hôtel de Paris are worth a look too.

INFORMATION

🔲 D2

🏠 2a boulevard des Moulins (☎ 0377 92 16 61 16; www.monaco-tourisme.com)

🔁 Cap Ferrat (▶ 57), the Corniches (▶ 31), Èze (33), Menton (▶ 57), Nice (▶ 44)

Casino

✉ Place du Casino

☎ 0377 98 06 20 00; www.casino-monte-carlo.com

🕐 Mon–Fri from 2pm, Sat, Sun from noon

❓ Over 18s only. Passport required

🚌 1, 4, 6

♿ Good

💶 Expensive

Monaco's splendid casino dominates place du Casino

39

Montagne Ste-Victoire

INFORMATION

➕ B2

ℹ️ Aix-en-Provence Tourist
Office: 2 place du
Général-de-Gaulle
(☎ 04 42 16 11 61; www.
aixenprovencetourism.com)

🔄 Aix-en-Provence (► 25)

❓ The path to the summit
may be closed Jul–Sep
due to fire risk

*Acres of vines flourish in
the range of which
Montagne Ste-Victoire is
the highest peak (top).
The huge rocky mountain
of Montagne Ste-Victoire
(below)*

**Paul Cézanne was so fascinated by
Montagne Ste-Victoire that he painted
it over 65 times, making this Provençal
landmark famous worldwide.**

The Montagne Ste-Victoire lies just east of Aix-
en-Provence. Viewed end on, this 16km long
silvery ridge (running east–west) takes the form
of a shapely pyramid. On its lower red-soil
slopes, Coteaux-d'Aix vineyards give way to
dense forest, scrub and fragrant herbs. Above
the treeline, the limestone peak reflects every
hue of light and shadow – blue, grey, white,
pink, orange – creating extraordinary designs on
the landscape.

For Paul Cézanne, native of Aix, the
mountain was his favourite local subject. He
painted it again and again from all angles and at
all hours, creating some of his greatest canvases,
including *La Montagne Sainte-Victoire* (1904) and

Le Paysage d'Aix (1905). In a letter
to his son in 1906, he wrote 'I
spend every day in this landscape,
with its beautiful shapes. Indeed,
I cannot imagine a more pleasant
way or place to pass my time.'
Climbing Montagne Ste-Victoire
requires stout shoes and sure-
footedness as, although not the
highest mountain in Provence, it
is said to be the steepest. It is a
steady two-hour hike from les
Cabassols on the D10 to the
ruined 17th-century priory and
massive Croix de Provence at the
945m summit. At the eastern
base of the mountain is
Pourrières wood, where the
mountain was named following a
Roman victory over invading
Germanic tribes.

Musée Marc-Chagall, Nice

Chagall was a highly individualistic Russian-Jewish painter who drew his main themes from the Old Testament and Russion folklore.

Located in the heart of a Mediterranean garden at the foot of Cimiez hill, this striking modern museum was specially designed by André Hermant to house Marc Chagall's 'Biblical Message' – a series of 17 monumental canvases, created between 1954 and 1967, evoking the Garden of Eden, Moses and other Old Testament themes. The museum was opened by the artist himself in 1973. Chagall also created the mosaic of the prophet Elijah, cleverly reflected in the pool, and the beautiful blue stained-glass windows representing *The Creation of the World* in the concert hall. Other works, including paintings, etchings, lithographs, sculptures and tapestries, were donated to the museum after Chagall's death in 1985, making this the most important permanent collection of his work.

INFORMATION

🔳 D2
✉ Avenue Docteur-Ménard
☎ 04 93 53 87 20;
www.musee-chagnall.fr
🕐 Jul–Sep Wed–Mon 10–6;
Oct–Jun 10–5. Closed 1
Jan, 1 May, 25 Dec
🍴 Garden café Apr–Oct (€)
🚌 15
♿ Excellent
💰 Moderate
🔗 Musée Matisse (► 42)
❓ Shop, library, concert
hall. Reserve guided tours
in advance

Inside the modern exterior (above) visitors marvel at Marc Chagall's distinctive works (below)

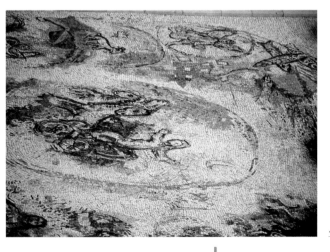

Musée Matisse, Nice

A truly remarkable collection of Matisse's works, intimate yet instructive and spanning his entire life, housed in a vivid red villa.

INFORMATION

- D2
- 164 avenue des Arènes-de-Cimiez
- 04 93 81 08 08; www.musee-matisse-nice.org
- Wed–Mon 10–6. Closed Tue and public hols
- 15, 17, 20, 22, 25
- Very good
- Moderate
- Musée Marc-Chagall (➤ 41)
- Guided tours. Shop

The vivid-red façade of the Musée Matisse (above) with modern additions (below)

MATISSE

The Villa des Arènes is situated on a hill above Nice, at the heart of a 3.6-hectare olive grove in the district of Cimiez – an exquisite mid-17th-century folly, with a cleverly-painted *tromp l'oeil* façade, colonnaded staircases and terraces that are laid out in the Genoese style.

Henri Matisse first came to live in Nice in 1917 and spent long periods of his life near here. Shortly before his death in 1954 he bequeathed his entire personal collection to the city of Nice. Together with a second, even larger donation from his wife in 1960 (including over a hundred personal effects from his studio-apartment in the nearby Hôtel Regina), it formed the basis of a priceless collection, celebrating the life, work and influence of this great artist, and boasting not only the world's largest collection of his drawings, but also all the bronze sculptures that Matisse ever made.

Matisse's entire life is displayed in the villa, from the old-master copies he made during his apprenticeship period, through an era of sober, dark-toned paintings in the 1890s (including *Intérieur à l'harmonium*), to his Impressionist and Fauvist phases (*Jeune femme à l'ombrelle* and *Portrait of Madame Matisse*), and beyond to the bright colours and simple shapes of his maturity, best protrayed in his decorative paper cut-outs, silk-screen hangings and works such as *Nu Bleu IV* and *Nature Morte aux Grenades*.

The large collection of his drawings and engravings (around 450 altogether) are also of particular interest. Do not miss the book illustrations for James Joyce's *Ulysses* and the powerful sketches and stained-glass models for the Chapelle du Rosaire at Vence.

Musée Picasso, Antibes

Picasso once had a studio inside this seafront château. Today it houses one of the world's finest collections of his works.

The Grimaldi dynasty ruled for centuries in this beautiful 12th- to 16th-century château, constructed following the design of a Roman fort and occupying a strategic site overlooking the ramparts. In 1928, the city of Antibes acquired the castle to house a museum of art, history and archaeology. When, in 1946, Pablo Picasso returned to his beloved Mediterranean, having spent the war years in Paris, he found that he had nowhere suitable to work. The mayor of Antibes lent him a room in Château Grimaldi for use as an atelier and in gratitude Picasso left his entire output of that period on permanent loan to the castle museum, together with a collection of lively ceramics, tapestries and sculptures that he later created in the nearby village of Vallauris.

Although Picasso only spent six months in Antibes, it was one of his most prolific periods. After the melancholy of war, his work here took on a new dimension, reflecting the *joie de vivre* of the Mediterranean, bathed in sunny colours and incandescent light. He combined bold new techniques – using industrial paints, fibro-cement and plywood – with ancient themes and mythical images, creating such masterpieces as *Le centaur et le Navire*, *Ulysee et les Sirènes*, *Nu couché au lit bleu* and his famous *La Joie de Vivre*.

Most of Picasso's works are on the first floor of the castle. Works by his contemporaries, including Fernand Léger and Max Ernst, hang on the second floor (Picasso's former studio), and the ground floor contains photographs of the great master at work. On a terrace overlooking the sea, stone and bronze sculptures by Mirò, Richier and Pagès are strikingly displayed among cacti, trees and flowers.

INFORMATION

➕ D2
✉ Château Grimaldi, place Mariéjol
☎ 04 92 90 54 20
🕐 Closed for restoration until early 2008 (phone for details)
💶 Moderate
🔄 Cagnes-sur-Mer (➤ 56), Cannes (➤ 54)

Sculptures mounted on the museum's ramparts (above). Grounds of the 12th-century château where the collection is housed (below)

Nice

INFORMATION

🔲 D2
ℹ 5 promenade des Anglais
(☎ 08 92 70 74 07;
www.nicetourisme.com)

Despite being France's largest tourist resort, Nice remains a friendly place, full of Mediterranean character, with its own identity and a unique past.

Only unified with France in 1860, Nice retains a strong Italianate character, combining Italian temperament and lifestyle with French finesse and *savoir faire*. By the 1860s, the city had become Europe's most fashionable winter retreat, and exuberant belle-époque hotels sprang up along the fashionable Promenade des Anglais. As its name suggests, this palm-lined promenade, which graciously sweeps round the Baie des Anges (Bay of Angels), was constructed at the expense of Nice's wealthy English residents in 1822 so they could stroll along the shoreline. Today it is bordered by a highway of *autoroute* proportions and the white wedding cake-style architecture of the luxury belle-époque hotels, such as the world-famous Negresco (► 73), are now juxtaposed with ugly concrete apartment blocks.

Nearby, the alleyways and markets of the *vieille ville* contrast boldly with the broad boulevards and designer shops of the modern city around the handsome main square, place Masséna. Old Nice is a maze of dark, narrow streets, festooned with flowers and laundry and brimming with cafés, hidden squares and bustling markets. Cours Saleya is a spacious, sunny square and the scene of one of France's top fruit and vegetable markets. By night, cafés and restaurants fill the cours, making it one of Nice's most animated night spots.

This delightful setting has attracted many artists over the years. As a result, Nice is blessed with more museums and galleries than any French town outside Paris. The best include the Musée d'Art Moderne (► 50), Musée Marc-Chagall (► 41) and Musée Matisse (► 42).

Cours Saleya (top). The magnificent Russian orthodox church (above) built by Tsar Nicolas II in 1903

Roussillon

It is easy to fall in love with Roussillon, once known worldwide for its ochre dyes, now considered one of France's most beautiful villages.

INFORMATION

🖪 B1
🖪 Place de la Poste
(☎ 04 90 05 60 25;
www.roussillon-
provence.com)
↔ The Lubéron (▶ 37)
🅿 Ochre festival held in May
(during Ascension
weekend)

This unforgettable village is perched on a platform of rich rust rock called Mont Rouge, surrounded by jagged cliffs and hollows of every shade of ochre imaginable from blood red, gold, orange and pale yellow to white, pink and violet, hidden amid dark pine forests and scrub. For here lie the richest deposits of ochre in all France.

The village of Roussillon was founded by Raymond d'Avignon. According to legend, one day he discovered his wife was having an affair with his page-boy. He killed the page and served his heart on a platter to his wife. Greatly distressed, she leapt off the cliffs: her blood formed a spring, permanently colouring the surrounding soil and creating some of the most spectacular scenery in the whole of Provence, from the spiky multicoloured needles of the 'Valley of Fairies' to the brilliantly hued 'Cliffs of Blood' and deep gullies of the 'Giant's Causeway'. Here visitors can explore the old opencast quarries along the 1km *Sentier des Ocres* (Ochre Trail), which has information signboards along the way.

The ochre industry began here in the late 18th century, bringing prosperity to the villagers until 1958, when competition from cheap synthetic pigments forced production to stop. Today, few quarries are worked, but Roussillon still holds its Ochre Festival at Ascensiontide.

The picturesque houses present a full palette of ochre shades that create a special glow in the streets. The hub of the village is the small square beside the Mairie, where locals gather in the outdoor cafés. Narrow lanes and winding stairways lead up to a Romanesque church, offering a panorama of the Vaucluse scenery.

Brightly coloured ochre quarries (top) encase the village of Roussillon. Stone from the quarries is used to build the houses here (above)

St-Tropez

INFORMATION

🔲 C3
🔲 Quai Jean-Jaurès
  (☎ 04 94 97 45 21;
  www.ot-sainttropez.com)
🔲 Port-Grimaud (► 54)

Even though the hedonistic image of St-Tropez in the 1960s has grown jaded, this little fishing port continues to seduce the rich and famous.

Most visitors come to St-Tropez to rub shoulders with the glitterati in the waterfront cafés, and admire the grandiose yachts, moored before a backdrop of pink and yellow pastel buildings. These are relatively modern, reconstructed from original designs after the destruction that occurred during World War II. Take time to explore the narrow streets and medieval squares of old St-Tropez, where you will find a village of great character, with its colourful markets, chic boutiques and romantic bistros.

Founded by Greeks as Athenopolis (City of Athena), the town has long been a popular meeting place for artists. Liszt and Maupassant were its first celebrities in the 1880s, followed by neo-Impressionist painter Signac a decade later. Soon Matisse, Bonnard, Utrillo and Dufy fell under St-Tropez's spell, immortalising the town in paint. Many pictures can be seen in the Musée de L'Annonciade (► 50). An influx of writers arrived between the wars, including Colette and Cocteau. Then, in the 1950s, it was the turn of the film stars, led by the famous Tropézienne, Brigitte Bardot. Her scandalous film, *Et Dieu Créa La Femme* (*And God Created Woman*) of 1956, marked the start of a permissive era and the Bardot/St-Tropez cult.

Today, the waterfront is very much the place to see and be seen in St-Tropez, so try to arrive in your Aston Martin, on your Harley Davidson, or better still in an enormous floating gin palace, and remember to moor stern-to, giving onlookers a good view! It's fun to wander along the quayside, to marvel at the size and cost of these ostentatious yachts and to watch their millionaire owners partying on deck.

St-Tropez's busy waterfront (top) is a magnet for pleasure craft and fishing boats.
Église St-Tropez (above)

Théâtre Antique, Orange

One of the best surviving theatres from the ancient world, built over 2,000 years ago, with seating for up to 10,000 spectators.

The Théâtre Antique was built in the reign of Augustus about AD 1, set into the hillside of Colline St-Eutrope at Arausio. Originally there had been a Celtic settlement here, but under Caesar, veterans of the second Gallica legion created a major Roman city, building the magnificent theatre, the triumphal arch, temples, baths and many other public buildings.

Although all that remains of the theatre is a mere shadow of its former splendour, it is easy to imagine the theatre in its heyday. The *cavea*, or tiered semicircle, was divided into three levels according to rank. On one tier you can still see the inscription *EQ GIII* meaning 'Equus Gradus III' or 'third row for horsemen'. Senators and guests of honour would occupy marble seats in front of the first row.

The monumental stage wall (*frons scanae*), made from red sandstone and measuring 103m long, 37m high and nearly 2m thick, is the only one in the world to survive completely from ancient times. Louis XIV described it as 'the greatest wall in my kingdom'. Once decorated with 76 columns, friezes, niches and statues, today all the statues have vanished except an imposing marble figure of Emperor Augustus. Beneath the statue is the central 'Royal door', and within the wall were hidden passageways enabling actors and stagehands to move about unseen. For the same purpose the wooden stage had numerous trap doors. Its excellent acoustics are demonstrated every July and August in the Chorégies, a world-famous festival of opera, drama and ballet, held here since 1869. Classical, jazz and pop concerts are also held here throughout the summer.

INFORMATION

- ➕ A1
- ✉ Rue Madeleine Roch
- ☎ 04 90 51 17 60; www.theatre-antique.com
- 🕐 Jan, Feb, Nov, Dec 9.30–4.30; Mar, Oct 9.30–5.30; Apr, May, Sep 9–6; Jun–Aug 9–7
- ♿ Restricted
- 💷 Moderate
- ❓ Guided tours available

Orange's amphitheatre, an awesome sight to behold (top). Standing alone, Augustus above the entrance to the auditorium (above)

47

Vaison-la-Romaine

One of Provence's best-preserved Roman sites, Vaison is an unusual blend of modern town, medieval village and former Roman city.

The richness of Vaison's past only emerged in the 20th century when excavations unearthed extensive Roman remains, including the vast Maison des Messii, with its colonnaded courtyard and mosaic floors, and a Roman theatre (used for the July arts festival). The ruins lie in two halves on either side of place Abbé Sautel. To the east is the Quartier de Puymin, and on the other side of the road, excavations are still going on in the Quartier e la Villasse. Visit the Roman city before crossing the 2,000-year-old Pont Romain over the jade-green Ouvèze river to the *haute ville*.

Clinging to a lofty jagged rock above the river, the sand-coloured houses of Vaison's medieval village, draped with knotted vines, creepers and pomegranate bushes, have been lovingly restored by artists and craftsmen. It is a steep climb to the ruined 13th-century château through a maze of twisting cobbled streets, rewarded by wonderful views across the Ouvèze Valley as far as the snow-topped Alps.

The extensive ruins cover an area of 13 hectares (top). Tiers of the Roman theatre's auditorium built into the hillside (right)

PROVENCE & THE CÔTE D'AZUR's best

Museums

MUSÉE GRANET

Aix-en-Provence's main museum, housed in the Gothic priory of the Knights of Malta, contains 19th-century Aixois artist François Granet's collection of French, Italian and Flemish paintings. After refurbishment, a new group of modern works – some by Picasso – was added in 2007.

➕ B2 ✉ Place St-Jean-de-Malte, Aix-en-Provence
☎ 04 42 52 8832
🕐 Wed–Mon 12–6
🎟 Inexpensive 🚹 Good

Stark lines and white structures create the Musée d'Art Moderne, Nice

In the Top 25

🔟 FONDATION MAEGHT, ST-PAUL-DU-VENCE (► 34)
1️⃣8️⃣ MUSÉE MARC-CHAGALL, NICE (► 41)
1️⃣9️⃣ MUSÉE MATISSE, NICE (► 42)
2️⃣0️⃣ MUSÉE PICASSO, ANTIBES (► 43)

MUSÉE ANGLADON

This museum, in an elegant city mansion, boasts the prestigious collection of artists Jean and Paulette Angladon-Dubrujeaud, including paintings by Sisley, Manet, Cézanne and Picasso, and Provence's only original van Gogh.

➕ A1 ✉ 5 rue du Laboureur, Avignon ☎ 04 90 82 29 03; www.angladon.com 🕐 Wed–Sun 1–6. Also open Tue from mid-Apr to mid-Oct 🎟 Moderate

MUSÉE DE L'ANNONCIADE

This former 16th-century chapel houses one of the finest collections of French late 19th- and early 20th-century paintings and bronzes. St-Tropez was then one of the most active centres of avant-garde art and, as a result, much of the 100 or so canvases here belong to the great movements of pointillism, Fauvism and Nabism. Many of the paintings portray local scenes. Look for Paul Signac's *L'Orage* (1895), Bonnard's *Le Port de St-Tropez* (1899), Camoin's *La Place des Lices* (1925), works by Dufy, Derain, Vuillard and others – and the museum cat, called Matisse!

➕ C3 ✉ Place Georges-Grammont, St-Tropez ☎ 04 94 97 04 01 🕐 Jun–Sep Wed–Mon 10–11, 3–7; Oct–May 10–12, 2–6. Closed Nov, 1 Jan, 1 May, Ascension, 25 Dec 🚹 Few 🎟 Moderate

MUSÉE DE L'ARLES ANTIQUE

This splendid museum is an absolute must see. It is built over the Cirque Romaine, an enormous 2nd-century chariot racecourse, which has recently been excavated. It is a modern museum covering the history of the area from Roman rule to the Christian era.

➕ A2 ✉ Presqu'île du Cirque-Romain, Arles ☎ 04 90 18 88 88; www.arles-antique.cg13fr 🕐 Apr–Oct 9–7, Nov–Mar 10–5. Closed hols 🚹 Excellent 🎟 Moderate

MUSÉE D'ART MODERNE

The museum's collections trace the history of French and American avant-garde art from the 1960s to the present: new realists, American pop art, minimalism and the Nice School, in particular its founder Yves Klein. The building, itself a 'museum-monument', is a masterpiece of modern architecture, with fine views from its rooftop terraces.

➕ D2 ✉ Promenade des Arts, Nice ☎ 04 97 13 42 01;

www.mamacnice.org 🕐 Tue–Sun 10–6. Closed Mon and hols
🚌 5, 6, 7, 81, 82, 88, 89 🍽 Cafés & restaurants ♿ Excellent
💶 Moderate

MUSÉE OCÉANOGRAPHIQUE

Monaco's prestigious Oceanographic Museum was
founded by Prince Albert I in 1910 to house his
remarkable collections of marine flora, fauna, nautical
instruments and a 20m whale skeleton. This
spectacular aquarium and museum of marine science
is the finest of its kind in the world. It is located in a
grandiose building on a sheer cliff high above the
Mediterranean. Marine explorer Jacques Cousteau
set up his research centre here and his remarkable
films are regularly screened in the museum's cinema.
The 'Sharks Lagoon' is a recent welcome addition to
the museum.

✚ D2 ✉ Avenue St-Martin, Monaco ☎ 0377 93 15 36 00;
www.oceano.mc 🕐 Oct–Mar 10–6; Apr–Jun, Sep 9.30–7; Jul, Aug
9.30–7.30 🍽 Restaurant & bar 🚌 1, 2 ♿ Good 💶 Expensive

MUSÉE DU PETIT PALAIS

The beautifully restored former residence of the
bishops of Avignon was converted in 1958 to house
two important collections – medieval works from the
Musée Calvet and the Campana collection of 13th-
to 16th-century Italian paintings from the Louvre.
The medieval works include 600 sculptures and
around 60 paintings, such as the *Retable Requin* by
Enguerrand Quarton.

✚ A1 ✉ Place du Palais du Papes, Avignon ☎ 04 90 86 44 58
🕐 Oct–May 9.30–1, 2–5.30; Jun–Sep 10–1, 2–6. Closed Tue, 1 Jan,
1 May, 14 Jul, 1 Nov, 25 Dec ♿ Few 💶 Moderate

PALAIS DU ROURE

Until the end of the last century, this Florentine-style
palace was the office of Frédéric Mistral's Provençal-
language magazine *L'Aïoli*. Today it is a beautiful
museum of Provençal history, arts, literature and
traditions.

✚ A1 ✉ 3 rue du Collège-du-Roure, Avignon ☎ 04 90 80 80 88
🕐 Guided tours Tue at 3pm; daily in Jul ♿ Few 💶 Moderate

GRASSE MUSEUMS

The famous perfumeries of
Fragonard, Molinard and
Galimard may be the main
draw to Grasse but, after you
have done the obligatory tour
of the perfume factories, there
are several museums clustered
nearby worth seeking out. The
Fragonard perfumery has a
museum in the same building,
with a wonderful collection of
rare perfumery objects. Across
the street over the Fragonard
shop, the Musée Provençal du
Costume et du Bijou has local
costumes and jewellery from
the 18th and 19th centuries.
The Musée International de
la Parfumerie (closed for
restoration) houses works by
the rococo Jean-Honoré
Fragonard. There is also the
Musée d'Art et d'Histoire de
Provence, which displays
Provençal decorative arts and
furniture.

*Don't be fooled by the
contemporary exterior –
the Musée de l'Arles
Antique is full of history
inside*

Historical Sites

CHATEAU D'IF

This forbidding fortress castle lies 3km offshore on the barren, rocky Île du Frioul, near Marseilles. Its long history represents an extraordinary blend of fact, fiction and legend. Built in 1528 by François I to protect the port, it later became a prison, with famous inmates including the legendary *Man in the Iron Mask* and also Alexander Dumas' fictional *Count of Monte Cristo*.

➕ B3 ☎ 04 91 59 02 30 🕐 Daily 9.30–5.30 or 6.30. Closed Mon Sep–Mar 🍴 Café 🚢 Quai des Belges (☎ 04 91 46 54 65) ♿ Few 🎫 Moderate

Chateau d'If, near Marseille

LES ALYSCAMPS

According to custom, the Roman necropolis of Alyscamps (Latin *Elisii Campi*, Elysian Fields) was built outside the city walls along the Via Aurelia. Christians took over the cemetery and several miracles are said to have taken place here, including the appearance of Christ. Burial here was so sought after that the dead were sealed in barrels and floated down the Rhône to Arles with a piece of gold between their teeth for the gravedigger. Formerly, the necropolis had 19 chapels and several thousand tombs – all that remains is a tranquil alleyway lined with poplar trees and moss-covered tombs.

➕ A2 ✉ Avenue des Alyscamps, Arles ☎ 04 90 49 38 20 🕐 Daily 9–7. Closed hols ♿ Good 🎫 Moderate

ARÈNES

Built during the 1st century AD, this was the largest amphitheatre in Gaul (136m long and 107m wide), able to seat over 20,000 spectators and scene of blood-thirsty contests between gladiators and wild animals. Originally it had three storeys, each with 60 marble-clad arcades, and an awning to protect the audience from the elements. During the Middle Ages, the stones from the third level were used to build two churches and 200 houses inside the arena to shelter the poor. These were demolished in 1825, leaving the amphitheatre once again free for bullfights.

➕ A2 ✉ Rond-Point des Arènes, Arles ☎ 04 90 49 38 20 🕐 May–Oct 9–6.30; Mar, Apr, Oct, Nov 9–6; Dec–Feb 10–5. Closed 1 Jan, 1 Nov, 25 Dec and for occasional bullfights ♿ Few 🎫 Moderate

CATHÉDRALE ST-SAUVEUR

Aix's main church combines a variety of architectural styles: the baptistery is 5th-century, the cloisters Romanesque, the transept and chancel Gothic and the main portal has magnificently carved walnut Renaissance doors. Don't miss Nicolas Froment's famous triptych *Le Buisson Ardent* (1475–6), depicting a vision of the Virgin and Child surrounded by the eternal burning bush of Moses.

➕ B2 ✉ 34 place des Martyrs-de-la-Résistance, Aix-en-Provence 🕐 Daily 9–12, 2–5 ♿ Good

PALAIS DES PAPES

The majestic, monumental Pope's Palace was built in a spacious cobbled square as a symbol of the papal residency in Avignon. Its massive walls shelter a labyrinth of halls, courtyards and chambers divided into the Old Palace, built by Pope Benedict XII between 1334 and 1342, and the New Palace, begun under his successor, Pope Clement VI and completed in 1348. Each part has its own distinctive character. Benedict XII's Old Palace has an almost austere, monastic simplicity in stark contrast with the New Palace. Clement VI enjoyed the high life and was an ardent patron of the arts, displaying his wealth and power in lavish frescoes and flamboyant ceilings. His ostentatious New Palace received a mixed reception. Medieval chronicler Froissart pronounced it 'the finest and strongest palace in the world', whereas Petrach called it 'Unholy Babylon … a sewer where all the filth of the universe has gathered'. The entire complex is so vast that it has been described as 'a city within a city' and takes at least a day to visit. Don't miss the fanciful Audience Hall, the frescoes of the Stag Room, the princely papal bedroom, St Martial's Chapel and the Hall of the Consistory.

🔼 A1 ✉ Place du Palais, Avignon ☎ 04 90 27 50 00; www.palais-des-papes.com 🕐 Mid-Mar to Jul, Oct 9–7; Aug–Sep 9–8; Nov to mid-Mar 9.30–5.45 🍴 Café in summer months ♿ Few 💰 Expensive; inclusive ticket with Pont St-Bénézet ❓ Guided tours ☎ 04 90 27 50 73

PALAIS DU PRINCE

In summer, when Prince Albert is away, guided tours take visitors through the priceless treasures of the State Apartments and the small Musée Napoléon in the south wing of the palace. When he is in residence, the royal colours are flown from the tower and visitors must content themselves with the Changing of the Guard ceremony (daily at 11.55am).

🔼 D2 ✉ Place du Palais, Monaco ☎ 0377 93 25 18 31; www.palais.mc 🕐 May–Oct 9.30–6.30; Nov 10–5.30; Apr 10.30–6 🚌 1, 2 ♿ None 💰 Moderate

PONT ST-BÉNÉZET

Projecting from the city wall by the Porte du Rhône is one of Avignon's most photographed landmarks. This bridge, which has been made famous in the popular children's song *Sur le pont d'Avignon*, was one of the first bridges built across the Rhône. Originally made of wood, it was reconstructed in stone at the end of the 13th century. Only four of its original 22 arches remain, together with the tiny chapel of St Nicholas on the second pier. The song by an anonymous composer is famous worldwide. However, it was under the arches of the bridge (*sous le pont*), on the Île de la Barthelasse, that the people of Avignon used to dance.

🔼 A1 ✉ Rue Ferruce, Avignon ☎ 04 90 27 51 16; www.palais-des-papes.com 🕐 Mid-Mar to Jul, Oct 9–7; Aug–Sep 9–8; Nov to mid-Mar 9.30–5.45 ♿ None 💰 Expensive; inclusive ticket with Palais des Papes

ST-TROPEZ CITADELLE

Visit this 16th-century hilltop fortress if only for the view, which embraces the orange, curly-tiled roofs of St-Tropez's *vieille ville*, the dark and distant Maures and Esterel hills, and the glittering blue of the bay, flecked with sails. The Citadelle contains a naval museum (closed for restoration), illustrating the town's long and glorious history, right up to the 1944 Allied landings that destroyed so much of the town.

🔼 C3 ✉ Montée de la Citadelle

The cloisters of Cathédrale St-Sauveur, Aix-en-Provence

Hill Towns & Villages

ENTREVAUX

Sleepy Entrevaux was once an important border defence between France and Savoy, heavily fortified in the 1690s by Vauban, Louis XIV's military architect. Enter the village across a drawbridge, through one of three gatehouses into a hotchpotch of typical Provençal medieval houses, surprisingly untouched by the proximity of the Alps. The steep zig-zagging path to the mighty citadel that tops the ensemble is well worth the climb for the views of the Haut-Var and the surrounding mountains beyond.

➕ C1 ℹ️ Porte Royale du Pont Levis (☎ 04 93 05 46 73) ❓ Tourist office open summer only

A river flows gently through the peaceful village of Fontaine-de-Vaucluse

BORMES-LES-MIMOSAS

Despite a chequered history – founded by the Gauls, conquered by the Romans, then sacked by Saracens, Corsairs, Moors, Genoese and finally during the Wars of Religion – this hillside village remains one of the prettiest of the entire coast. Its ice-cream-coloured houses spiral down steep stairways and alleys, with amusing names – Lover's Lane (Venelle des Amoreux), Gossipers Way (Draille des Bredovilles) and steepest of all, Bottom-Breaker Road (Roumpi-Cuou)! Depending on the season, Bormes is bathed in the scent of mimosa, eucalyptus and camomile. In February, when the mimosa is in full bloom, it celebrates with its sensational *corso fleuri* – an extravaganza of floral floats made from a myriads tiny yellow flowers.

➕ C3 ℹ️ 1 place Gambetta (☎ 04 94 01 38 38; www.bormeslesmimosas.com)

FONTAINE-DE-VAUCLUSE

Tucked away at the end of the narrow enclosed valley, after which the whole Vaucluse *département* is named, Fontaine-de-Vaucluse is famous for its emerald-green spring, which gushes from a huge cave-like abyss at the foot of a 230m cliff. Research has proved this is one of the world's largest and most powerful springs. It consists of a vast underground labyrinth of rivers covering over 2,000sq km and is able to produce up to 200,000 litres of water per second at certain times of year. Pagan Gauls believed it to be the home of a god, while Christians named it the Devil's Hole.

➕ A1 ℹ️ Chemin de la Fontaine (☎ 04 90 20 32 22)

GRIMAUD

One of Provence's most photogenic *villages perchés*, Grimaud is crowned by a romantic 11th-century château belonging to the Grimaldi family, after whom the village is named. By contrast, Port-Grimaud on the coast is a modern mini-Venice of ice-cream-coloured designer villas lining the quayside. Designed by François Spoerry in the 1960s, it is best viewed by water taxi (*coche d'eau*) or from the church tower.

➕ C3 ℹ️ 1 boulevard des Alziers, Grimaud (☎ 04 55 43 83; www.grimaud-provence.com) ❓ Tourist train links Port-Grimaud to the hilltop village of Grimaud

MOUSTIERS-STE-MARIE

Dramatically perched high on a ridge surrounded by sheer cliffs, Moustiers marks the start of the great gorges of the Verdon river (► 36). In the 17th and 18th centuries, its white decorated earthenware pottery was famous throughout the world. Now *Faïence de Moustiers* has been revived and is sold in countless craft shops in every cobbled square. The 5th-century chapel of Notre-Dame-de-Beauvoir is pinned against the rockface at the top of the village. Above it hangs a renowned gold star, suspended on a 227m chain, presented to the village by a knight called Blacas to celebrate his release from captivity during a crusade.

➕ C2 ℹ️ Place de l'Église (☎ 04 92 74 67 84)

ORANGE

Historic Orange, the 'Gateway to Provence', lies in the fertile plain of the Rhône river. Its main claim to fame are two of the finest Roman monuments in Europe – the great triumphal arch and the Théâtre Antique (► 47). Today, Orange is an important centre for Côtes du Rhône wines and olives, honey and truffles. The massive 22m Arc de Triomphe was built around 20BC. It was constructed as a symbol of Roman power following Caesar's conquest of the Gauls and victory over the Greek fleet; its three archways are covered with intricate carvings depicting naked Gauls bound in chains, victorious Roman legionaries and a variety of nautical symbols portraying maritime supremacy. Originally constructed along the Via Agrippa from Lyon to Arles, today it stands on a roundabout in the middle of the N7.

➕ A1 ℹ️ 5 cours Aristide-Briand (☎ 04 90 34 70 88; www.otorange.fr)

ST-RÉMY-DE-PROVENCE

Warm peaches-and-cream-coloured buildings, the maze of lanes, the fountains, the squares and the tree-lined boulevards portray the true flavour of Provence. Nostradamus was born here in 1503, but today St-Rémy owes its popularity to van Gogh, who convalesced in an asylum south of town after his quarrel with Gauguin and the ear-cutting incident in Arles. He produced 150 canvases and over 100 drawings during his one year's stay here, including *Starry Night*, *The Sower* and his famous *Irises*. Near the asylum lie the extensive remains of the wealthy Greco-Roman town of Glanum, the oldest classical buildings in France. The area was first settled in 6BC and the city was abandoned in the 3rd century when it was overrun by barbarians. Buildings nearby, called Les Antiques, were also part of the Roman town: the oldest and smallest triumphal arch in France, dating from 20BC and the best-preserved mausoleum of the Roman world, erected as a memorial to Caesar and Augustus.

➕ A2 ℹ️ Place Jean-Jaurès (☎ 04 90 92 38 52; www.saintremy-de-provence.com)

ST-PAUL-DE-VENCE

Gently draped over a hill close to Cagnes, this picture-postcard *village perché* was appointed a 'Royal Town' in the 16th century by King François. Today it is a tourist honeypot, with coachloads flocking to the Fondation Maeght (► 34) and the smart shops and galleries. Yet despite the crowds it remains one of Provence's most beautiful villages, especially at night when the narrow alleys are lit with tiny lanterns.

➕ D2 ℹ️ Maison de la Tour, 2 rue Grande (☎ 04 93 32 86 95)

Moustiers-Ste-Marie clings to the banks of the Rioul river at the base of craggy cliffs

Coastal Towns & Resorts

In the Top 25

ST-TROPEZ (► 46)

CAGNES-SUR-MER

Cagnes is divided into three: the old fishing quarter and main beach area of Cros-de-Cagnes; Cagnes-Ville, the commercial centre with its smart racecourse beside the sea; and Haut-de-Cagnes. This inviting hilltop village, with its brightly coloured houses smothered in bougainvillea, mimosa and geraniums, is crowned by a 14th-century château, built by Admiral Rainier Grimaldi as a pirate lookout. Renoir spent the last 11 years of his life nearby at Domaine des Collettes, now the Musée Renoir. He would sit and paint beneath the olive trees, his brushes strapped to his rheumatic fingers.

➕ D2 ℹ 6 boulevard Maréchal-Juin (☎ 04 93 20 61 64; www.cagnes.tourisme.com)

Boats moored in Cannes' sheltered bay

ANTIBES

Antibes was founded in the 5th century BC as a Greek trading post, and centuries later was controlled by the dukes of Savoy until the 18th century. Today, its massive ramparts protect Old Antibes from flooding. Old Antibes, which lies hidden behind the ramparts, is a maze of cobbled, winding lanes overflowing with shops, restaurants and bars. Don't miss the bustling morning market in cours Masséna. On the waterfront, the Port Vauban yacht harbour attracts some of the Riviera's most luxurious yachts.

➕ D2 ℹ 11 place du Général-de-Gaulle (☎ 04 97 23 11 11; www.antibesjuanlespins.com)

CANNES

Think Cannes, think movies and film stars, expensive boutiques, palatial hotels and paparazzi! After all, it is twinned with Beverly Hills and, within France, second only to Paris for shopping, tourism and major international cultural and business events, including the world-famous film festival (► 22). With so much glitz, it is easy to forget that Cannes was a mere fishing village until 1834, when retired British chancellor Lord Brougham was enchanted by its warm climate and quaint setting and built a villa here to spend the winter months. Soon hundreds of other aristocrats and royals followed his example. However, it was not until the 1930s that Cannes became a summer resort and by the 1950s mass summer tourism had taken off. The Vieux Port and the old Roman town of Canois Castrum (now known as le Suquet) occupy a small hill to the west, crowned by an 11th-century castle and watchtower affording a sweeping coastal vista. To the east, modern Cannes is built round la Croisette, an elegant sea promenade lined with palms and flanked by grand belle-époque hotels and golden beaches, each with their tidy rows of coloured parasols and mattresses.

➕ D2 ℹ Palais des Festivals, 1a Croisette (☎ 04 93 39 24 53; www.cannes.fr)

CASSIS

This cheerful little fishing port and beach resort basks in a sheltered bay between the cliffs of the Cap Canaille, Europe's highest sea cliffs, and the breathtaking *calanques* to the west (► 29). The surrounding hills are smothered with olives, almonds, figs and the famous terraced vineyards of the region's highly reputed white wine. In the village centre, boccia players meet in dusty squares while fishermen spread their nets along the bustling quayside, beside its colourful waterfront cafés.

🔸 B3 ℹ️ Quai des Moulins (☎ 0892 259 892; www.ot-cassis.com)

MENTON

Just 1.6km from the border, France's most Italianate resort, with its steep jumble of tall, honey-coloured houses, is wedged between a sweeping palm-lined bay and a dramatic mountain backdrop. Menton is France's warmest town, resulting in a town bursting with semi-tropical gardens. Menton is also the 'lemon capital of the world', smothered in citrus groves. In February, a spectacular Lemon Festival takes place in the Jardins Biovès. The medieval old town has two magnificent churches and a beautiful old cemetery with striking sea views. Other notable sights include the Musée Jean-Cocteau, the Musée de la Préhistoire Régional, boasting the remains of 'Menton Man' (30,000BC) and the sumptuous 18th-century summer residence of the princes of Monaco, now Menton's main art museum.

🔸 D2 ℹ️ Palais de L'Europe, 8 avenue Boyer (☎ 04 92 41 76 76; www.menton.com)

STES-MARIES-DE-LA-MER

This picture-postcard fishing village is steeped in the tradition and folklore of the Camargue (➤ 30), with its whitewashed cottages, colourful costumes, bullfights and flame-red sunsets. According to legend, the Virgin Mary's half-sisters Maria Jacobé and Maria Salome landed here in AD40 with their black serving maid Sarah, patroness of gypsies. When they died a chapel was built over their graves and the village has been a place of pilgrimage ever since. The pilgrimage takes place in May. Gypsies carry statues of the Marias and the bejewelled black Sarah in a small blue boat into the sea to be blessed, led by mounted *gardiens* in full Camargue cowboy dress. There then follows a sparkling festival of bullfighting, flamenco and fireworks.

🔸 A2 ✉️ 5 avenue Van-Gogh (☎ 04 90 97 82 55; www.saintesmaries.com)

CAP-FERRAT

The most desirable address on the Côte d'Azur – the 'Peninsula of Billionaires', with its huge villas hidden in subtropical gardens – has long been a favourite haunt of the rich and famous, including King Leopold II of Belgium, Somerset Maugham, Edith Piaf, the Duke and Duchess of Windsor, Charlie Chaplin and David Niven. A delightful coast path from Villefranche around the cape past countless tiny azure inlets (ideal for a refreshing dip) makes a pleasant stroll before lunch in the former fishing village of St-Jean-Cap-Ferrat. Cap-Ferrat's finest villa – considered by many the finest on the Riviera – is the Villa Ephrussi de Rothschild, a rose-pink belle-époque palace constructed by the flamboyant Baroness Béatrice Ephrussi de Rothschild (1864–1934), set in immaculate formal gardens with wonderful sea views. The remarkable interior is lavishly decorated with rare furniture (including some pieces that once belonged to Marie Antoinette), set off by rich carpets, tapestries and an eclectic collection of rare *objets d'art*.

🔸 D2 ℹ️ 59 avenue Denis Semeria (☎ 04 93 76 08 90; www.ville-saint-jean-cap-ferrat.fr)

Fondation Ephrussi-de-Rothschild set among houses on the narrow neck of the Cap-Ferrat peninsula

57

Places to Take Children

SNOW FUN

Many of Provence's larger ski resorts offer excellent facilities for families with children of all ages, and a variety of winter sports: ice skating, husky-mushing, tobogganing, horse-drawn sleigh rides. The family resort of Orcières-Merlettes (☎ Tourist office 04 92 55 89 89) has a crèche for children and children's skiing lessons. Serre Chevalier and Isola 2000 (► 83) offer similar facilities.

An exhibit from the Musée de l'Automobiliste, Mougins

ANTIBES LAND

All ages will enjoy this amusement park, with over 30 thrilling attractions, including rollercoasters and water rides.

🔒 D2 ✉ Avenue Mozart, route N7, Antibes ☎ 04 93 33 68 05; www.azurpark.com 🕐 Apr to mid-Jun Sat–Sun 2pm–7pm; mid-Jun to Aug daily 8.30pm–1am (Sat from 4pm, Sun 3pm); Sep Sat–Sun 4pm–2am 🖐 Expensive

AQUACITY

Children are happy to splash away countless hours in this aquatic paradise of pools and water games.

🔒 B3 ✉ 13240 Septemes-les-Vallons (off Aix–Marseille autoroute), Marseille ☎ 04 91 51 54 08; www.aquacity.fr 🕐 Jun–Sep 10–6/7 🖐 Expensive

AZUR PARK

Twenty-eight exhilarating attractions for both children and adults.

🔒 C3 ✉ Gassin, Golfe de St-Tropez ☎ 04 94 56 48 39; www.azurepark.com 🕐 Apr 4pm–midnight; May 7pm–midnight; Jun–Aug 8pm–1am; Sep 8–midnight 🖐 Expensive

FORMULE KART'IN

Indoor go-karting circuit for children (aged 7 upwards) and adults.

🔒 D2 ✉ 215 avenue Francis-Tonner (RN7), Cannes ☎ 04 93 47 88 88 🕐 Mon–Sat 5.30–12.30, Sun 2–8 🖐 Expensive

FUN KART

Go-karting for children and adults, just outside Grasse.

🔒 C2 ✉ Plateau de la Sarée (Route de Gourdon) ☎ 04 93 42 48 08; www.fun-karting.com 🕐 Daily 9.30–6 🖐 Expensive

GROTTES DE ST-CÉZAIRE

Fairy-tale world of rich red caves filled with 'musical' stalactites and stalagmites in magical shapes.

🔒 C2 ✉ St-Cézaire-sur-Siagne ☎ 04 93 60 22 35 🕐 Oct to mid-Nov, Mar–May daily 2.30–5; Jun, Sep 1.30–12, 2–6; Jul, Aug 10.30–6.30; mid-Nov to Feb Sat–Sun 2.30–5 🖐 Expensive

MASSALIA THÉÂTRE

Language proves no barrier when children's favourite fairy tales come alive here.

🔒 B3 ✉ 41 rue Jobin, Marseille ☎ 04 95 04 95 70; www.theatremassalia.com 🚌 49A, 49B

MUSÉE DE L'AUTOMOBILISTE

Older children enjoy visiting the unique, radiator-shaped car museum, with its large collection of old and new cars and footage of classic races.

🔒 D2 ✉ 772 chemin de Font-de-Currault, Mougins ☎ 04 93 69 27 80 🕐 Daily 10–6/7 🖐 Moderate

MUSÉE NATIONAL

A huge collection of dolls dating from the 18th century
to Barbie.

🔲 D2 ✉ 17 avenue Princesse-Grace, Monaco ☎ 0377 93 30 91
26; www.monte-carlo.mc/musee-national 🕐 Oct–Easter, 10–12.15,
2.30–6.30; Easter–Sep, 10–6.30. Closed 1 Jan, 1 May, 19 Nov, 25 Dec
🎫 Moderate

PARC ZOOLOGIQUE LA BARBEN

Modern zoo with spacious enclosures for elephants,
giraffes, tigers and white rhinos. Picnic area and
playground.

🔲 B2 ✉ Route D572, between Salon-de-Provence and Aix-en-
Provence ☎ 04 90 55 19 12; www.zoolabarben.com 🕐 Daily 10–6
🎫 Moderate

LA PETITE PROVENCE

A typical, if a little idealised, Provençal village re-
created in miniature, showing daily scenes at school,
the market and in the café.

🔲 A2 ✉ Avenue de la Vallée-des-Baux, Paradou ☎ 04 90 54 35
75; www.lapetiteprovence.com 🕐 Daily 10–6.30 (7 Jul, Aug)
🎫 Moderate

LES TERRASSES DE FONTVIEILLE

An impressive collection of vintage cars, a naval
museum, a zoo – and even a McDonald's!

🔲 D2 ✉ Terraces de Fontfieille, Monaco ☎ Zoo 0377 93 25 18
31; naval museum 0377 92 05 28 48; classic car exhibition 0377 92 05
28 56 🕐 Zoo Oct–May daily 10–12, 2–5/6; Jun–Sep 9–12. 2–7.
Naval museum and classic car exhibition daily 10–6 🎫 Various prices

TIKI III

See the bulls, horses and wild birds of the Camargue
on a 90-minute mini cruise aboard a paddle boat.

🔲 A2 ✉ D38, 1.5km from Saintes-Maries-de-la-Mer ☎ 04 90 97
81 68 🕐 Phone for times

VILLAGE DES TORTUES

A fascinating one-hour tour of this remarkable 'village'
with its 1,200 turtles and
tortoises.

🔲 C3 ✉ 83590 Gonfaron (off
Aix–Cannes autoroute) ☎ 04 94
78 26 41; www.villagetortues.com
🕐 Mar–Oct daily 9am–6pm
🎫 Moderate

VISIOBULLE

Discover the underwater
world of 'Millionaire's
Bay' in a glass-bottomed
boat. Reservations
recommended.

🔲 D2 ✉ Embarcadère
Courbet, Juan-les-Pins ☎ 04 93 67 02 11; www.visiobulle.com
🕐 Apr–Jun, Sep departures at 11, 1.30, 3 & 4.30; Jul, Aug at 9.30,
10.25, 11.50, 2, 3.25, 4.50 & 6.15 🎫 Moderate

MARINELAND

A wonderful world of
performing sea lions, killer
whales and dolphins, and
close underwater encounters
with sharks (safely, within a
transparent tunnel!). Younger
children enjoy the pony tours,
face painting and stroking the
animals at La Petite Ferme du
Far West. Older children hurtle
down the Aqua-Splash water
slides and mum and dad try
their hand at crazy-golf. All
this and more at Marineland.

🔲 D2 ✉ 306 avenue
Mozart, route N7, Antibes
☎ 04 93 33 49 49;
www.marineland.fr 🕐 Daily
10–7 (until midnight Jul, Aug)
🎫 Expensive

*Elephants at play, Parc
Zoologique la Barben*

Places to Have Lunch

You are spoilt for choice when it comes to having lunch in the sunshine

L'ANE ROUGE (€€–€€€)
Sample the catch of the day at this highly rated Niçoise restaurant overlooking the port.
➕ D2 ✉ 7 quai des Deux Emmanuel, Nice ☎ 04 93 89 49 63

CAFÉ DE FRANCE (€–€€)
Escape to the hills and eat such local delights as rabbit with mustard, served on a large, vine-covered terrace.
➕ C3 ✉ Place Neuve, Grimaud ☎ 04 94 43 20 05

CHEZ CÉSAR (€€)
One of the few places on the waterfront where you can try Cassis' famous fresh seafood at a reasonable price.
➕ B3 ✉ 21 quai des Baux, Cassis ☎ 04 42 01 75 47

CHEZ FONFON (€€–€€€)
Try the bouillabaisse here. Overlooking the fishing harbour east of Marseille.
➕ B3 ✉ 140 Vallon des Auffes, Marseille ☎ 04 91 52 14 38; www.chez-fonfon.com

L'ESCONDUDO (€€)
Hidden in the steep back streets; the delicious food is served on a sunny patio with the scent of mimosa.
➕ C3 ✉ 4 ruelle du Moulin, Bormes-les-Momosas ☎ 04 94 71 15 53

LE GIRELIER (€€–€€€)
This port-side favourite is ideal for a light seafood lunch, plus prime people-watching.
➕ C3 ✉ Quai Jean-Jaurès, St-Tropez ☎ 04 94 97 03 87

LE MOULIN À HUILE (€€€)
Eat regional dishes with an innovative slant on a veranda beside the river.
➕ A1 ✉ Quai Marechal Foch, Vaison-la-Romaine ☎ 04 90 36 20 67; www.moulin-huile.com

LE NID D'AIGLE (€€)
Shady terraces among stone passages and steep cobbled alleyways provide an ideal tranquil spot for lunch.
➕ D2 ✉ 1 rue du Château, Èze village ☎ 04 93 41 19 08; www.leniggaigle.fr

LE VIEUX MOULIN (€€€)
A lovely old stone mill at the base of this beautiful *village perché*. Tasty Provençal specialities.
➕ D2 ✉ Route de Vence, St-Paul-de-Vence ☎ 04 93 32 10 45

PROVENCE &
THE CÔTE D'AZUR
where to...

Vaucluse

PRICES

Approximate prices for a three-course meal for one without drinks or service:
€ = under €25
€€ = €25–€50
€€€ = over €50

The restaurants on the following pages are all open for lunch and dinner daily unless otherwise stated.

A MEAL IN PROVENCE

'By 12.30 the little stone-walled restaurant was full. There were some serious stomachs to be seen…The proprietor of the restaurant… quivered with enthusiasm as he rhapsodised over the menu: foie gras, lobster mousse, beef *en croûte*, salads dressed in virgin oil, hand-picked cheeses, desserts of a miraculous lightness, *digestifs*. It was a gastronomic aria which he performed at each table.'
(*A Year in Provence* by Peter Mayle)

AVIGNON

LE BELGOCARGO (€)
Belgian restaurant offering 16 types of *moules frites* on a huge sunny terrace.
✉ 10 place des Châtaignes
☎ 04 90 85 72 99 ⏰ Closed Sun, Mon except Jul, Aug

CHRISTIAN ÉTIENNE (€€€)
One of Avignon's gourmet temples in a 14th-century palace beside the Palais des Papes. Try the fish, foie gras and truffle specialities.
✉ 10 rue de Mons ☎ 04 90 86 16 50 ⏰ Closed Sun, Mon

LE CLOÎTRE (€)
Savoury or sweet pancakes washed down with a bowl of cider, in a cosy traditional restaurant.
✉ 9 place du Cloître-St-Pierre
☎ 04 90 85 34 63 ⏰ Closed Sun, Mon

LA FOURCHETTE (€€)
A smaller, more relaxed, cheaper offspring of Hiély-Lucullus (► below), but still with delicious dishes. Very popular. Reservations essential.
✉ 17 rue Racine ☎ 04 90 85 20 93 ⏰ Closed Sat, Sun

HIÉLY-LUCULLUS (€€€)
Avignon's top gastronomic palace, rated as one of France's top 50 restaurants.
✉ 5 rue de la République
☎ 04 90 86 17 07;
www.hiely.net

LE PETIT BEDON (€€)
A lively restaurant, popular with the local students, which serves hearty portions of Provençal cuisine and robust local wines. Good value set menu at lunchtime.
✉ 70 rue Joseph-Vernet
☎ 04 90 82 33 98
⏰ Closed Sun

SIMPLE SIMON (€)
This quaint olde-worlde English tea room serves steak and kidney pie, Bakewell tart and even Christmas pudding.
✉ 26 rue Petite-Fusterie
☎ 04 90 86 62 70
⏰ Closed Sun, Mon

BONNIEUX

LE FOURNIL (€€)
A rustic restaurant at the heart of the Lubéron, with a charming fountain-splashed terrace for al-fresco dining.
✉ 5 place Carnot ☎ 04 90 75 83 62 ⏰ Closed Mon, Tue, Dec, Jan

CAVAILLON

PRÉVOT (€€€)
Chef Jean-Jacques Prévot's lavish dining room is matched by equally rich cuisine. Try his *artichaut soufflé* and his succulent Cavaillon melon desserts.
✉ 353 avenue Verdun
☎ 04 90 71 32 43;
www.restaurant-prevot.com
⏰ Closed Sun, Mon

CHÂTEAUNEUF-DU-PAPE

LA MÈRE GERMAINE (€€)
One of the the village's most popular restaurants. The wine list includes the best *crus* of the appellation.

✉ Avenue du Commandant-Lemaître ☎ 04 90 83 54 37; www.lameregermaine.com
🕐 Closed Tue dinner, Wed in winter

GORDES

LE MAS TOURTERON (€€€)
A true taste of Provence in an 18th-century farmhouse, courtesy of Elisabeth Bourgeois' imaginative and refined regional cuisine.
✉ Chemin St-Blaise, Lles-Imberts ☎ 04 90 72 00 16; www.mastourteron.com
🕐 Sun lunch only. Closed Mon, Tue Nov–Mar

LOURMARIN

LE MOULIN DE LOURMARIN (€€€)
Four extravagant menus in a beautiful old oil mill. A feast for the senses.
✉ Rue du Temple ☎ 04 90 68 06 69 🕐 Closed Tue, Wed lunch, Jan–Feb

MÉNERBES

LE GALOUBET (€€)
Exquisite regional cuisine served in a small, cheerful dining room or al-fresco under the olive trees.
✉ 104 avenue Marcellin Poncet ☎ 04 90 72 36 08; www.moulindelourmarin.com

MONTEUX

LE SAULE PLEUREUR (€€€)
Exceptional regional cooking from one of the Maîtres Cuisiniers de France.
✉ 145 chemin de Beauregard, Monteux (near Carpentras)

☎ 04 90 62 01 35 🕐 Closed Sat lunch, Sun dinner, Mon

ORANGE

LE YACA (€)
Provençal bistro with wooden beams, floral tablecloths, generous portions and a jolly atmosphere near the Théâtre Antique.
✉ 24 place Sylvian ☎ 04 90 34 70 03 🕐 Closed Wed, Tue dinner in winter, Nov

ROUSSILLON

DAVID (€€€)
Admire the red cliffs of ochre from the terrace of this delightful restaurant. Wholesome Provençal cuisine.
✉ Place de la Poste ☎ 04 90 05 60 13; www.tablesdecharme.com 🕐 Closed Wed, Sun dinner

SÉGURET

LE MESCLUN (€€)
Intimate restaurant serving regional dishes, washed down with Côtes-du-Rhône wines. Sweeping views of the Comtat Venaissin.
✉ Rue des Poternes ☎ 04 90 46 93 43; www.lemesclun.com 🕐 Closed Mon, Tue

VENASQUE

AUBERGE DE LA FONTAINE (€–€€)
Cosy log fire in winter and classical concerts once a month. Try the *gigot d'agneau de Venasque* and other local dishes.
✉ Place de la Fontaine ☎ 04 90 66 02 96; www.auberge-la-fontaine.com 🕐 Dinner only. Closed Wed

MAÎTRES CUISINIERS

Provence and the Côte d'Azur has more than its fair share of Master Chefs (Maîtres Cuisiniers de France) – an elite association of top chefs devoted to preserving the art of French cuisine. They include Michel Philibert (Le Saule Pleureur, ▶ 63), Christian Étienne (Christian Étienne, ▶ 62), Alain Burnel (L'Oustau de Baumanière, ▶ 65), Claude Girard (Les Santons, ▶ 66) and Christian Willer (La Palme d'Or, ▶ 68).

Bouches-du-Rhône

A PRICKLY PLATEFUL

Don't be surprised if you are presented with a plate of shiny, black, seaweed-draped *oursin* (sea urchins), as they are considered a great delicacy in Cassis. Simply scrape out the rosy-pink insides and eat raw with a glass of the prestigious *vin de Cassis*. Legend has it that God felt sorry for the people of Cassis and shed a tear which landed on a vine, giving birth to a dry white wine of a pale green tint, with a bouquet of heather and rosemary.

AIX-EN-PROVENCE

AUTOUR D'UNE TARTE (€)

The generous slices of sweet and savoury tarts featured here make a perfect snack. Takeaway also available.

✉ 13 rue Gaston de Saporta
☎ 04 42 96 52 12
🕐 Closed Sun

LA BROCHERIE (€€)

Try one of the meat dishes, spit-roasted in the large chimney, or the fish at this rustic restaurant. Also delicious game in season.

✉ 5 rue Fernand-Dol
☎ 04 42 38 33 21; www.restaurantlabrocheriepaysaix.com
🕐 Closed Sat lunch, Sun

CAFÉ LES DEUX-GARÇONS (€€)

'Les 2 G' was founded in 1792, and was once the haunt of Cézanne, Picasso, Piaf and Zola. Today, still with its original mirrors and chandeliers, it remains one of Aix's most elegant cafés, popular with locals and visitors alike for its brasserie-style menu.

✉ 53 cours Mirabeau
☎ 04 42 26 00 51; www.les2garcons.com

JACQUOU LE CROQUANT (€)

Tasty *tourtons* (wholewheat pancakes) with different fillings in an intimate non-smoking bistro.

✉ 2 rue de l'Aumône-Vieille
☎ 04 42 27 37 19; www.jacquou.com 🕐 Closed Mon, Sun in winter, Sun lunch in summer

LA MAISON DES FONDUES (€€)

You will find 50 varieties of fondue here, from the traditional *bourguignone* to chocolate and chestnut cream dips.

✉ 13 rue de la Verrerie
☎ 04 42 63 07 78; www.maisondesfondues.com
🕐 Dinner only

AU PAIN QUOTIDIEN (€)

The first Provençal outlet of a growing chain of bakery-cafés, with a country-kitchen feel. Breads, jams, condiments, ciders and coffees to buy. The open sandwiches, quiches, soups, salads and pâtisseries make an ideal lunch snack.

✉ 5 place Richelme
☎ 04 42 23 48 57

UNIC BAR (€)

A perfect bar for people-watching, opposite Aix's colourful fruit and vegetable market. In summer, fresh fruit juice is the speciality.

✉ 40 rue Vauvenargues
☎ 04 42 96 38 28
🕐 6am–2am

YAMATO (€€)

An authentic and reasonably priced Japanese restaurant.

✉ 21 avenue des Belges
☎ 04 42 38 00 20; www.restaurant-yamato.com
🕐 Closed Tue lunch, Mon

ARLES

L'AFFENAGE (€€)

Traditional fare in the converted stables of an 18th-century coaching inn.
✉ 4 rue Molière ☎ 04 90 96 07 67 🕐 Closed Sun

L'ESCALADOU (€)

Authentic, down-to-earth Arlésien restaurant packed with locals. Hearty helpings of *aïoli* (garlic mayonaise), Arles sausages and *boeuf gardian*.

✉ 23 rue Porte-de-Laure
☎ 04 90 96 70 43

LA PAILLOTTE (€)

The decor may be simple, but the menu includes fine Provençal flavours and local wines.

✉ 28 rue du Dr-Fanton
☎ 04 90 96 33 15

LES BAUX

L'OUSTAU DE BAUMANIÈRE (€€€)

One of France's finest hotel-restaurants, visited by royalty, politicians and celebrities.

✉ Val 'Enfer ☎ 04 90 54 33 07; www.oustaudebaumaniere.com ⊙ Closed Jan–Feb, Wed in winter

CASSIS

LA VOUTE (€)

A heaped pan of *moules frites* washed down with *vin de Cassis* on the waterfront. Excellent value.

✉ 2 quai des Baux ☎ 04 42 01 73 33

EYGALIÈRES

LE BISTROT D'EYGALIÈRES 'CHEZ BRU' (€€)

The imaginative country cooking in this small village restaurant includes pigeon served with foie gras. Delicious.

✉ Rue de la République
☎ 04 90 90 60 34 ⊙ Closed

Mon, Sun dinner Oct–May, Jun–Sep Tue lunch as well

MARSEILLE

LE MAS DE LULLI (€)

Early birds meet night owls here for a coffee and a snack at dawn.

✉ 4 rue Lulli ☎ 04 91 33 25 90 ⊙ Open 24 hours. Closed Aug

LE MIRAMAR (€€€)

The ultimate bouillabaisse beside the old port (► panel).

✉ 12 quai du Port ☎ 04 91 91 10 40; www.bouillabaisse.com ⊙ Closed Mon, Sun ⊕ Metro (Vieux Port)

TOINOU (€–€€)

Home of Francis Rouquier, France's champion shellfish opener.

✉ 3 cours St-Louis ☎ 04 91 33 14 94; www.toinou.com
🚌 31, 33, 34, 41, 80, 81

ST-RÉMY-DE-PROVENCE

CAFÉ DES ARENES (€)

A small bar-cum-restaurant serving tasty local cuisine. Try a bull steak followed by crème brûlée with thyme. The pavement terrace enjoys the evening sun.

✉ 9 boulevard Gambetta
☎ 04 90 92 13 43
⊙ Closed Tue

CAFÉ DES ARTS (€)

Join the locals in St-Rémy's most popular restaurant, with its steak and frogs' legs.

✉ 30 boulevard Victor-Hugo
☎ 04 90 92 08 50 ⊙ Closed Tue, Feb

BOUILLABAISSE

This world-famous fish soup originated in Marseille as a nourishing family meal, made with choice fish kept aside by the fishermen especially for their families. It is traditionally made with up to a dozen different kinds of fish, cooked in a stock containing saffron, herbs and fennel. It is served with croutons, which are smeared with *rouille* (a sauce of fresh red chilli peppers crushed with garlic and olive oil), sprinkled with cheese, then dunked in the soup.

65

Var & Haute-Provence

'IN' WITH THE JET SET

Here are some tips on where to be seen during your stay in St-Tropez. For breakfast, Sénéquier's Salon de Thé (⊠ Quai Jean Jaurès) is a must. Moules is on the lunchtime menu at Café des Arts, place des Lices' number one address. Le Grand Joseph (⊠ 1 place de l'Hôtel de Ville) is currently 'in' for brunch and dinner, and the notorious Tropezien institution, Le Gorille (⊠ Quai de Suffren) remains the place to eat steak tartare after the nightclubs close at dawn.

BORMES-LES-MIMOSAS

L'ESCOUNDUDO (€€)
Enjoy wholesome regional dishes flavoured with herbs from the surrounding hills, on a sunny terrace, hidden in a steep back alley.
⊠ 4 ruelle du Moulin ☎ 04 94 71 15 53 🕙 Closed Sat, Sun out of season

LOU PORTAOU (€€)
Hidden in a picturesque corner of Bormes, this small restaurant serves a simple menu of market-fresh Provençal cuisine. The set menus are very good value.
⊠ 1 rue Cubert ☎ 04 94 64 86 37 🕙 Closed lunch Jun–Oct, Tue mid-Nov to mid-Dec

COLLOBRIÈRES

LA PETITE FONTAINE (€)
Try some local delicacies of the Massif des Maures, washed down with wine from the local cooperative on a shady terrace. Peaceful.
⊠ 1 place de la République ☎ 04 94 48 00 12 🕙 Closed Sun dinner, Mon, 2 weeks Sep

DIGNE-LES-BAINS

LE GRAND PARIS (€€)
With the reputation of Digne's best restaurant, in a former 17th-century convent. Try the pigeon accompanied by courgette flowers cooked in the juice of truffles.
⊠ 19 boulevard Thiers ☎ 04 92 31 11 15; www.hotel-grand-paris.com 🕙 Closed Mon, Tue lunch Dec–Feb

FAYENCE

LE CASTELLERAS (€€€€)
Frog's legs wrapped in pastry with cream and chives is one of many local specialities served in this old stone *mas*.
⊠ Route de Seillans ☎ 04 94 76 13 80; www.restaurant-castelleras.com 🕙 Closed Mon, Tue

GAP

LE TOURTON DES ALPES (€€)
The local speciality of *tourtons* – tiny hot pastry envelopes filled with either potato, spinach, meat, prune or apple – are served here in copious quantities.
⊠ 1 rue des Cordiers ☎ 04 92 53 90 91

GRIMAUD

LES SANTONS (€€)
Classic cuisine and impeccable service in elegant Provençal surroundings. Les Santons is most definitely one of the region's top restaurants.
⊠ Route Nationale 558 ☎ 04 94 43 21 02 🕙 Closed Wed, Thu lunch, Nov–Mar

LES ISSAMBRES

VILLA SAINT-ELME (€€€)
One of the coast's most spectacular restaurant terraces, with exceptional cuisine to match. Try the lobster tart followed by *pigeon en croûte*.
⊠ Corniche des Issambres ☎ 04 94 49 52 52; www.saintelme.com

MOUSTIERS-STE-MARIE

LA BASTIDE DE MOUSTIERS (€€)

Dine in the country home of the world's top chef, Alain Ducasse. Despite the reputation, it remains surprisingly affordable (► panel).

✉ Chemin de Quinson, 04360 la Grisolière ☎ 04 92 70 47 47; www.bastide-moustiers.com ⏰ Closed Mon–Wed Jan–Mar, 16–26 Jan

LES SANTONS (€€)

Widespread reputation for good food and a pretty setting.

✉ Place de l'Église ☎ 04 92 74 66 48 ⏰ Closed Tue, mid-Sep to mid-Jan

ST-TROPEZ

BISTRO DES LICES (€€)

Robust flavours combined with a gentle touch is the reason why this fashionable bistro still manages to flourish even though it is away from the busy port area.

✉ 3 place des Lices ☎ 04 94 55 82 82

LA BOUILLABAISSE (€€)

A speciality fish restaurant in a traditional fisherman's cottage on the beach.

✉ Quartier la Bouillabaisse ☎ 04 94 97 54 00 ⏰ Closed mid-Oct to mid-Feb

CAFÉS DES ARTS (€€)

A favourite haunt of the see-and-be-seen brigade since the 1960s. You come for the fun, not the food (► 66, panel).

✉ Place des Lices ☎ 04 94 97 02 25 ⏰ 8am–midnight

LA CITADELLE (€€)

This tiny, atmospheric restaurant spills out on to the street. Don't miss the *tarte tatin*.

✉ 1 rue Aire du Chemin ☎ 04 94 54 81 19 ⏰ Apr–Sep 12–2, 7–10.30

L'EAU A LA BOUCHE (€–€€)

Simple, home cooking on a sunny pavement terrace in a cobbled backstreet near the Chapelle de la Misericorde. Excellent value.

✉ 43 rue du Portail Neuf ☎ 06 19 73 42 53

LA TABLE DU MARCHÉ (€–€€)

This smart bistro offers Provençal specialities from chef Christophe Leroy. Light snacks, pâtisseries and even afternoon tea are also available in the relaxed setting, with comfy chairs, bookshelves and warm regional hues.

✉ 38 rue Georges Clemenceau ☎ 04 94 97 85 20; www.christophe-leroy.com

SISTERON

HÔTEL RESTAURANT DE LA CITADELLE (€€)

Enjoy a spectacular alpine panorama whilst trying local delicacies such as *fougasse à l'anchois* (anchovy stuffed bread) or Sisteron lamb with thyme and rosemary. Eat on the terrace or in the dining room decorated with copper pots and landscape paintings.

✉ 126 rue Saunerie ☎ 04 92 61 13 52 ⏰ Closed Nov, Feb

ALAIN DUCASSE

Don't expect to find Monsieur Ducasse himself in the kitchen at La Bastide de Moustiers as he is far too busy looking after his restaurant in Paris, having left the famous Louis XV in Monaco (► 68). Instead he has entrusted the cooking to star pupil Monegasque Sonia Lee, who delights her guests with sensational dishes that embrace all the flavours and scents of Haute-Provence.

Alpes-Maritimes

NICE'S TOP CHEF

Irresistible local dishes such as *pâté au pistou* and *tripes Niçoise* are the trademarks of Dominic Le Stanc, former chef of the Negresco's famous Chantecler restaurant, and a name synonymous with the very best in Provençal cuisine. He now owns La Mérenda – a tiny rustic restaurant which he runs with his wife – a temple of Niçoise cuisine.

ANTIBES

LE BACON (€€€)
One of the coast's best fish restaurants, with exceptional views over old Antibes.
✉ Boulevard Bacon, Cap-'Antibes ☎ 04 93 61 50 02; www.restaurantbacon.com ⏰ Closed Mon, Tue lunch (except Jul–Aug), Nov–Mar

BIOT

LE JARRIER (€€)
Imaginative cuisine and an unmistakable Provençal flavour in an old jar factory.
✉ 30 passage de la Bourgade ☎ 04 93 65 11 68; www.lejarrier.com ⏰ Closed Tue, Wed

CANNES

LA PALME D'OR (€€€)
Join the stars at Cannes' most prestigious restaurant to experience some of prize-winning master chef Christian Willer's latest culinary creations, served in ornate surroundings..
✉ Hotel Martinez, 73 boulevard de la Croisette ☎ 04 92 98 73 00 ⏰ Closed Sun, Mon

ÈZE

LA BERGERIE (€€)
Traditional dishes with a good choice of Côtes-de-Provence wines. Winter by the open fire, summer on the shady terrace overlooking the sea.
✉ Grande Corniche Èze ☎ 04 93 41 03 67 ⏰ Dinner only, Sun lunch in summer. Closed Wed in winter

LA CHÈVRE D'OR (€€€)
Breathtaking sea views and inspired French cuisine.
✉ 3 rue du Barri ☎ 04 92 10 66 66; www.chevredor.com ⏰ Closed mid-Nov to Feb

HAUT-DE-CAGNES

LE SANT ELENA (€)
A small café-restaurant beside the castle that specialises in local dishes such as *mesclun* and *petits farcis*.
✉ 1 place Grimaldi ☎ 06 13 86 71 48

MONACO

LOUIS XV (€€€)
Should you break the bank at the Casino, come to the Louis XV, with its three Michelin rosettes.
✉ Hotel de Paris, place du Casino ☎ 0377 98 06 88 64; www.alain-ducasse.com ⏰ Closed Tue, Wed (except Wed dinner Jun–Aug), Dec and 2 weeks in Mar

ZEBRA SQUARE (€€)
Rub shoulders with the beautiful people on the sun terrace of this chic Mediterranean restaurant where even the crockery has zebra stripes.
✉ 10 avenue Princesse-Grace, Monte-Carlo ☎ 0377 99 99 25 50; www.zebrasquare.com

MOUGINS

LE MOULIN DE MOUGINS (€€€)
A bastion of Provençal cuisine, headed by celebrated chef Alain Llorca since 2004.
✉ Notre-Dame de Vie ☎ 04 93 75 78 24; www.moulin-mougins.com ⏰ Closed Mon

LES MUSCADINS (€€€)

A poor, young artist called Picasso stayed here once. To pay for his accommodation he painted murals on his bedroom walls, but the outraged owner made him whitewash over them. The pizzeria, Bellvista, serves delicious food on the terrace overlooking the bay or in a cosy dining room.

✉ 18 boulevard Courteline ☎ 04 92 28 43 43; www.hotel-mougins-muscadins.com ⏰ Closed Tue, Wed

NICE

APHRODITE (€€)

The imaginative culinary creations of chef David Faure are a seductive blend of classic French and Niçoise cuisine.

✉ 10 boulevard Duboncharge ☎ 04 93 85 63 53; www.restaurant-aphrodite.com ⏰ Closed Sun, Mon 🚌 38

CHANTECLER (€€€)

Nice's leading restaurant and a bastion of French gastronomy.

✉ Hôtel Negresco, 37 promenade des Anglais ☎ 04 93 16 64 00; www.hotel-negresco-nice.com ⏰ Closed Mon, Tue 🚌 11, 52, 59 94, 98

FENOCCHIO (€)

The best ice creams on the Côte d'Azur.

✉ Place Rossetti ☎ 04 93 80 72 52 ⏰ 9am–midnight 🚌 All buses to Gare Routière

FLO (€€)

Brasserie in a converted art-deco theatre with the kitchen on stage! Special late-night menu up to midnight.

✉ 4 rue Sacha-Guitry ☎ 04 93 13 38 38; www.flonice.com 🚌 1, 2, 5, 9, 10, 14, 22, 23

LA MÉRENDA (€€)

Irresistible menu of Niçoise specialities, prepared by one of France's outstanding chefs (► 68). No reservations.

✉ 4 rue de la Terrace ☎ No phone ⏰ Closed Sat, Sun, 2 weeks in Aug 🚌 All buses to Gare Routière ❓ Credit cards not accepted

LA PETITE MAISON (€€)

Local market-fresh dishes near the Opèra. The hors-d'oeuvres Niçoise is a meal in itself. Book well in advance.

✉ 11 rue St-François-de-Paule ☎ 04 93 92 59 59; www.lapetitemaison.com ⏰ Closed Sun 🚌 All buses to Gare Routière

LA ROTONDE (€)

The Riviera's most original brasserie. Bright merry-go-round decor complete with flashing lights, automats and painted wooden horses.

✉ Hôtel Negresco, 37 promenade des Anglais ☎ 04 93 16 64 00; www.hotel-negresco-nice.com 🚌 11, 52, 59, 94, 98

ST-PAUL-DE-VENCE

MAS D'ARTIGNY (€€€)

Well known for its *fruits de mer* and fish dishes. Not cheap, but the spectacular view makes it worth every euro. Inside a luxury spa hotel.

✉ Route de la Colle ☎ 04 93 32 84 54

LOU PILHA LEVA

'Lou Pilha Leva' in local Nissart patois means 'you take away'. At the heart of old Nice (✉ 10 rue du Collet), this hole-in-the-wall serves piping hot plates of *socca*, *pissaladière*, *beignets*, *farcis*, pizza and other Niçois specialities – €7 will buy you a bit of everything! Ideal for a snack lunch, the trestle tables provide the perfect opportunity to chat to the locals.

Vaucluse

PRICES

Prices are approximate for a double room, including breakfast:

€   = up to €60
€€   = €60–€130
€€€ = over €130

ÎLE DE LA BARTHELASSE

This island on the Rhône has had a colourful and varied history. Once a hunting reserve, it then became a gathering place of Avignonais prostitutes and thieves, but in later years it was a fashionable place to promenade and picnic. Today it is still a popular recreation site, with a lovely open-air swimming pool, campsites and several *chambres d'hôtes*.

APT

AUBERGE DU LUBÉRON (€€)

Apt's top hotel, beside the river.

✉ 8 place du Faubourg du Ballet ☎ 04 90 74 12 50; www.auberge-luberon-peuzin.com ⏲ Closed Nov

AVIGNON

AUBERGE DE CASSAGNE (€€€)

Ancient Provençal dwelling close to Avignon, with beautiful gardens, outdoor pool and a gastonomic restaurant.

✉ 450 allée de Cassagne, le Pontet ☎ 04 90 31 04 18; www.aubergecassagne.com

LA FERME (€)

Old farmhouse on the Île de la Barthelasse. Gypsy caravans in the garden are popular with actors during the summer festival.

✉ 110 chemin des Bois, Île de la Barthelasse ☎ 04 90 82 57 53 ⏲ Closed Nov to mid-Mar

LA MIRANDE (€€€)

Elegant hotel in a medieval palace, on a quiet cobbled square at the foot of the Popes' Palace.

✉ 4 place de l'Amirande ☎ 04 90 14 20 20; www.la-mirande.fr

BONNIEUX

DE L'AIGUEBRUN (€€)

A beautiful old, stone farmhouse 6km east of Bonnieux, peacefully located at the heart of the Lubéron National Park.

✉ Relais de la Canube ☎ 04 90 04 47 00; www.aubergedelaiguebrun.fr

GORDES

LE MAS DE LA BEAUME (€€)

A beautiful stone *mas* overlooking the village, with five rooms – each traditionally furnished with consummate taste. Picturesque garden and a fantastic farmhouse-style breakfast.

✉ 84220 Gordes Village ☎ 04 90 72 02 96; www.labeaume.com

MONTEUX

DOMAINE DE BOURNEREAU (€€)

This 250-year-old restored farm property is a veritable oasis of Provençal calm, which offers spectacular views of Mont Ventoux, 12 spacious, elegant rooms, extensive gardens and outdoor pool.

✉ 579 Chemin de la Sorguette ☎ 04 90 66 36 13; www.bournereau.com

ORANGE

ARÈNE KULM (€€)

Small three-star hotel in a quiet traffic-free square in the historic town centre.

✉ 8 place de Langes ☎ 04 90 11 40 40; www.hotel-arene.com ⏲ Closed mid-to late Nov

VAISON-LA-ROMAINE

HOSTELLERIE LE BEFFROI (€€)

Atmospheric hotel in Vaison's ancient *haute ville*.

✉ Rue de l'Evêché ☎ 04 90 36 04 71; www.le-beffroi.com ⏲ Closed Jan–Feb

Bouches-du-Rhône

AIX

DES AUGUSTINS (€€€)
Intriguing blend of history and modernity within a 15th-century former Augustinian convent.
✉ 3 rue de la Masse
☎ 04 42 27 28 59;
www.hotel-augustins.com

LE PIGONNET (€€€)
Beautiful family-run *bastide* hotel, with antique furniture, rose arbours and lovely views over the countryside.
✉ 5 avenue du Pigonnet
☎ 04 42 59 02 90;
www.hotelpigonnet.com

ARLES

ARLATAN (€€)
This charming 16th-century residence of the comtes d'Arlatan is one of the region's most beautiful historic hotels, with 30 rooms individually decorated with Provençal antiques.
✉ 26 rue Sauvage ☎ 04 90 93 56 66; www.hotel-artalan.fr

LE CALENDAL (€€)
Stylish Provençal mansion. Some rooms overlook the Roman arena.
✉ 5 rue Porte de Laure
☎ 04 90 96 11 89;
www.lecadendial.com

NORD-PINUS (€€€)
Unique hotel and a classified national monument. This is a hotel of strong literary connections, once a favourite haunt of the Félibres poets, and other literati, including Stendhal, Mistral, Cocteau and Henry James. Today it is popular with Christian Lacroix, top matadors and other wealthy aficionados, and is decorated accordingly with bull-fighting posters and trophies. Without doubt the place for people who want to feel truly Arlésien.
✉ Place du Forum ☎ 04 90 93 44 44; www.nord-pinus.com
🕐 Closed Jan–Mar

MARSEILLE

TONIC (€€€)
In an ideal spot at the western end of the Vieux Port, this chic hotel has modern, sound-proofed rooms; it's worth paying more for one with a view over the quayside.
✉ 43 quai des Belges
☎ 04 91 55 67 46 🚇 Metro (Vieux Port)

ST-RÉMY-DE-PROVENCE

HOTEL LES ATELIERS DE L'IMAGE (€€€)
An oasis of sophisticated minimalism at the heart of the town, with a tranquil garden, outdoor pool and an exotic restaurant.
✉ 36 Boulevard Victor Hugo
☎ 04 90 92 51 50;
www.hotelphoto.com

STES-MARIES-DE-LA-MER

HOTEL DE CACHAREL (€€)
A former *gardian* ranch in the heart of the marshes. Horse-riding and bull-watching.
✉ Route de Cacharel
☎ 04 90 97 95 44;
www.hotel-cacharel.com

LA CITÉ RADIEUSE

In 1952, architect Le Corbusier built a massive 17-storey concrete building intended to be part of a six-block Cité Radieuse (Radiant City), designed as a prototype for 'vertical living', combining living space, shops, schools and recreational facilities all under one roof. Sadly it looks far from radiant and Marseillais soon dubbed it the 'madman's house'.

Var & Haute-Provence

A HOTEL FOR ALL SEASONS

The exclusive Four Seasons Resort Provence at Terre Blanche, near Tourettes, comprises a series of modern deluxe villas gathered around a hilltop bar and restaurant area and leading down to two world-class golf courses and a clubhouse restaurant. There are also health and fitness suites, and superb business facilities – even broadband links beside each sunlounger at the swimming pool. Built on land formerly belonging to Sean Connery, the entire complex has been designed to resemble a Provençal village and offers a real getaway from the hustle and bustle of the Riviera.
☎ 04 94 39 90 00;
www.fourseasons.com/
provence

BORMES-LES-MIMOSAS

LE BELLEVUE (€)
A simple Logis de France establishment, with spectacular views to the sea.
✉ 12 place Gambetta
☎ 04 94 71 15 15;
www.bellevuebormes.fr.st
🕐 Closed Nov–Jan

COGOLIN

LA MAISON DU MONDE (€€)
This small, homely hotel with just 12 rooms, at the bustling heart of Cogolin, offers affordable accommodation for those wishing to worship the Tropezienne sun without paying St-Tropez prices There is.a pretty, shady garden and an outdoor pool for guests' use.
✉ 63 rue Carnot
☎ 04 94 54 77 54;
www.lamaisondumonde.fr

GRÉOUX-LES-BAINS

VILLA BORGHESE (€€)
A delightful hotel with colourful flower-filled balconies, a charming garden and pool.
✉ Avenue des Thermes
☎ 04 92 78 00 91;www.villa-borghese.com 🕐 Closed mid-Dec to mid-Mar

MONÊTIER-LES-BAINS

L'AUBERGE DU CHOUCAS (€€)
This cosy farmhouse, high in the Alps, is an ideal base for skiing at Serre Chevalier.
✉ Monêtier-les-Bains, 14km north of Briançon ☎ 04 92 24 42 73; www.aubergeduchoucas.com 🕐 Closed Nov to mid-Dec

ST-TROPEZ

CHÂTEAU DE LA MESSARDIERE (€€€)
St-Tropez's most luxurious hotel is truly palatial, and is sure to please.
✉ Route de Tahiti ☎ 04 94 56 76 00; www.messardiere.com 🕐 Closed Dec–Mar

MAS DE CHASTELAS (€€€)
Stay with Depardieu, Belmondo and other French film idols at this beautiful 18th-century *mas*, just outside St-Tropez.
✉ Quartier Bertaud, Gassin ☎ 04 94 56 71 71; www.chastelas.com 🕐 Closed weekdays Oct–Feb

VILLA MARIE (€€€)
On the hill overlooking Pampelonne, this chic boutique hotel and spa, stylishly decorated with terracotta, wrought iron and St Tropez azure, is the new address for the beautiful people.
✉ Route des Plages, Ramatuelle ☎ 04 94 97 40 22; www.villamarie.fr
🕐 Closed Nov–Apr

ST-VÉRAN

LES CHALETS DU VILLARD (€€)
Traditional alpine-style chalet accommodation in the highest village in Europe.
✉ St-Véran ☎ 04 92 45 82 08 🕐 Closed mid-Sep to mid-Dec, mid-Apr to mid-Jun

Alpes-Maritimes

CANNES

MARTINEZ (€€€)
Deluxe hotel with Cannes'
top restaurant, La Palme
d'Or (▶ 68).
✉ 73 boulevard de la Croisette
☎ 04 92 98 73 00; www.hotel-
martinez.com

CAP-D'ANTIBES

**HÔTEL DU CAP-EDEN-
ROC (€€€)**
Glorious hotel set in a park
on the top of the Cap.
Exquisite rooms and every
conceivable luxury.
✉ Boulevard J F Kennedy
☎ 04 93 61 39 01;
www.edenroc-hotel.fr ⏱ Closed
mid-Oct to mid-Apr

ÈZE

CHÂTEAU EZA (€€€)
A collection of medieval
houses, linked together to
form a luxury eagle's nest.
✉ Rue de la Pise ☎ 04 93
41 12 24; www.chateaueza.com

MONACO

HÔTEL DE PARIS (€€€)
Monte-Carlo's most
prestigious address.
✉ Place du Casino;
www.hoteldeparismontecarlo.com
☎ 0377 98 06 30 16

NICE

HÔTEL HI (€€)
Quirky hotel with wacky
furnishings, a hammam,
organic canteen and a
beach on the roof.
✉ 3 avenue des Fleurs ☎ 04
97 07 26 26; www.hi-hotel.net
🚌 38

NEGRESCO (€€€)
Famous hotel in the
belle-époque style with renowned restaurant (▶ 69)
✉ 37 promenade des Anglais
☎ 04 93 16 64 00; www.hotel-
negresco-nice.com 🚌 11, 52,
59, 94, 98, airport bus

**PALAIS MAETERLINCK
(€€€)**
Once the home of poet
Maurice Maeterlinck, now
a palatial, modern hotel.
✉ 30 boulevard Maurice-
Maeterlinck ☎ 04 92 00 72
00; www.palais-maeterlinck.com
🚌 14, 81

**PALAIS DE LA
MÉDITERRANÉE (€€€)**
Luxury seafront hotel
with 188 lavish rooms and
suites, a heated outdoor
pool and spa, and a
panoramic terrace.
✉ Promenade des Anglais
☎ 04 92 14 77 00; www.
lepalaisdelamediterranee.com
🚌 11, 52, 59, 94, 98,
airport bus

ST-JEAN-CAP-FERRAT

**GRAND HOTEL DU
CAP-FERRAT (€€€)**
Sumptuous palace in lush,
tropical gardens, amid
expensive real estate.
✉ 71 boulevard Géneral-de-
Gaulle ☎ 04 93 76 50 50;
www.grand-hotel-cap-ferrat.com

ST-PAUL-DE-VENCE

LA COLOMB D'OR (€€€)
Once a 1920s café where
Matisse and Picasso paid
for their drinks with
canvases. Now a deluxe
hotel.
✉ Place du Général-de-Gaulle
☎ 04 93 32 80 02; www.la-
colombe-dor.com

FAMOUS GUESTS

Charlie Chaplin taught his
children to swim in the pool
of the Grand Hôtel du Cap-
Ferrat. Queen Victoria was
one of the first famous
residents of the Hôtel de
Paris; Michael Jackson one
of the more recent.

Provençal Souvenirs & Gifts

A RAY OF SUNSHINE

Souleiado is a Provençal word meaning 'a sun-ray piercing through the clouds' and is the name of the leading manufacturer of block-printed Provençal textiles. The company was founded in 1938 by Charles Deméry in a successful attempt to revive a 200-year-old textile industry in Tarascon. The Musée Souleiado (✉ 39 rue Proudhon, Tarascon ☎ 04 90 91 50 11; www.souleiado-lemusee.com ⊙ Tue–Sat 10–1, 2–6) includes 40,000 18th-century fruitwood blocks which are still the basis for all the Souleiado patterns today.

ARLES

L'ARLÉSIENNE
Traditional Camarguais costumes.
✉ 12 rue du Président-Wilson
☎ 04 90 93 28 05

BIJOUTERIE PINUS
Necklaces, bracelets and crosses in traditional Provençal designs.
✉ 6 rue Jean-Jaurès
☎ 04 90 96 04 63;
www.bijoux-pinus.com

AUBAGNE

L'ATELIER D'ART
Manufacturer of faience and *santons* (small terracotta figures dressed or painted in regional costumes).
✉ 2 boulevard Émile-Combes
☎ 04 42 70 12 92

BIOT

VERRERIE DE BIOT
Traditional bubble-flecked glassware from Provence's capital of glass-blowing.
✉ Chemin des Combes
☎ 04 93 65 03 00;
www.verreriebiot.com

DIGNE-LES-BAINS

LA MAISON DE LA LAVANDE
Every imaginable lavender product is available here – they even sell a lavender liqueur.
✉ 38 boulevard Gassendi
☎ 04 92 31 33 94

GRASSE

PARFUMERIE FRAGONARD
The very finest perfumes from Provence. Visitors can take an interesting guided tour (► 51, panel) to learn more about the perfume industry.
✉ 20 boulevard Fragonard
☎ 04 93 36 44 65;
www.fragonard.com

MARSEILLE

LA COMPAGNIE DE PROVENCE
One of Marseille's few remaining specialist soap shops.
✉ 1 rue Caisserie ☎ 04 91 56 20 94 ⊛ Metro (Vieux Port)

NICE

PARFUMS POILPOT
Tiny, traditional perfumerie with a wide choice of scents from Grasse.
✉ 10 rue St-Gaëtan ☎ 04 93 85 60 77 ⊟ All buses to Gare Routière

ST-RÉMY-DE-PROVENCE

LES OLIVADES
Colour-drenched, printed fabrics, traditional Provençal clothing and gift ideas.
✉ 28 rue Lafayette ☎ 04 90 92 00 80

ST-TROPEZ

CHRISTOPHE GUERIN
See examples of Christophe Guerin's own unique style of painting in contemporary shades displayed along the waterfront.
✉ 4 rue Seillon ☎ 06 85 91 07 45

Fashion

AIX

PETIT BOY
Children's fashions from 6 months to 16 years.
✉ 6 rue Aude ☎ 04 42 93 13 05

ARLES

LA BOUTIQUE DU SAC
Buy an extra bag for all your souvenirs.
✉ 15 rue Josef Vernet ☎ 04 90 85 61 39

CHRISTIAN LACROIX
The boutique of the world-famous Arles-born designer (➤ panel).
✉ 52 rue de la République ☎ 04 90 96 11 16

MOURET CHAPELIER
One of France's few traditional milliners.
✉ 20 rue des Marchands ☎ 04 90 85 39 38

AVIGNON

SOULEIADO
Ladies who admire the Provençal-style clothes will be rather taken with Souleiado's ensembles (➤ panel).
✉ 5 rue Joseph-Vernet ☎ 04 90 86 47 67

BIOT

CHACOK
Bright colours and bold designs by Biot designer Arlette Chacok.
✉ 1050 Route de la Mer ☎ 04 93 65 60 60

MONACO

LANVIN
Designer Albert Elbaz brings a contemporary touch to the traditional mythic style of Jeanne Lanvin. Expect the VIP treatment at this elegant boutique next to the Jardin du Casino.
✉ Place du Casino ☎ 0377 93 50 46 61; www.lanvin.com

LOUIS VUITTON
This major name in the fashion world is just one of several equally famous on this road just around the corner from the Place du Casino.
✉ 6 avenue des Beaux Arts ☎ 0377 97 25 13 44

ROUSSILLON

GARANCE
Chunky multicoloured costume jewellery and fun fabric handbags.
✉ Place de la Mairie ☎ 04 90 05 81 57

ST-PAUL-DE-VENCE

BLEU COMME LÀ-BAS
A wacky, bright orange jewellery shop owned by a young, imaginative designer. Affordable and fun.
✉ 38 rue Grande ☎ 04 93 32 04 17

ST-TROPEZ

BLANC BLEU
Stylish, sporty fashion for both sexes.
✉ 3 rue Allard ☎ 04 94 97 66 94

HERMÈS
The ultimate in French chic.
✉ Place Grammont ☎ 04 94 97 04 29

LOCAL GENIUS

Christian Lacroix was born in Arles under the star sign of Taurus, the symbol of Camargue. One of haute-couture's most innovative and eclectic designers, his clothes are classic yet daring, feminine yet boldly Mediterranean, frequently inspired by the traditional Arlésian costumes. The fashions, jewellery, hats and handbags of his flamboyant boutique at the very heart of Arles' pedestrian zone represent a fashion mecca for the rich and fashionable.

Food & Drink

TOO MANY SWEETS GIVE YOU TOOTHACHE

The traditional souvenirs of Aix are its *calissons*, delicious almond and melon sweets first created in 1473 and still made in the traditional way by mixing ground almonds with glazed melons and fruit syrup. Beautifully packaged and best bought from Béchard or Riederer (✉ 67 cours Mirabeau), they make excellent presents (if you can resist eating them all yourself).

AIX

CHOCOLATERIE PUYRICARD

Puyricard's handmade chocolates are considered to be the finest in France. Visit their traditional chocolate factory in a northern suburb of Aix-en-Provence.

✉ 420 route du Puy, Sainte Reparade ☎ 04 42 96 11 21; www.puyricard.fr

MAISON BÉCHARD

An old-fashioned sweetshop, well known for its *calissons*.

✉ 12 cours Mirabeau
☎ 04 42 26 06 78

APT

APTUNION

Apt claims to be the world leader in crystallised fruits and this is the top shop in town. Phone in advance if you would like to arrange a factory tour.

✉ N100 (direction Avignon)
☎ 04 90 76 31 43;
www.kerryaptunion.com

AVIGNON

LES HALLES

This modern, covered farmers market is the perfect place to buy food for a picnic.

✉ Place Pie ⏰ Tue, Sun 7am–1pm

OLIVIERS & CO

Small but beautiful shop specialising in Provençal olives and their derivative products, including olive chutney, tapenades, oils and pastas.

✉ 19 rue Sainte Agricol
☎ 04 90 86 18 41

CANNES

CENERI

One of France's top cheese stores with over 300 different types, from huge rounds of runny brie to tiny *boutons de culotte* (trouser-button) goat's cheese.

✉ 22 rue Meynadier
☎ 04 93 39 63 68

L'ISLE-SUR-LA-SORGUE

LES DÉLICES DU LUBÉRON

A tasty selection of olive oil, tapenades, herbs, nougats, candies and other regional products.

✉ Avenue du Partage-des-Eaux
☎ 04 90 20 77 37

MARSEILLE

LE FOUR DES NAVETTES

This is Marseille's oldest bakery. Try the famous orange-flower *navette* biscuits, in the shape of the Stes Maries' legendary boat, originally only made for the Catholic feast day of Candlemas.

✉ 136 rue Sainte ☎ 04 91 33 32 12; www.fourdesnavettes. com 🚌 55, 61, 81

TORREFACTION NOAILLES

Mouth-watering sweetshop-cum-tea salon.

✉ 56 La Canebière ☎ 04 91 55 60 66 Ⓜ Métro 2 (Noailles)

MOURIÈS

MOULIN À HUILE COOPÉRATIF DU MAS NEUF

This unlikely looking

shed sells some of the best olive oil in France.

✉ Off D17 (direction Eyguières)
☎ 04 90 47 53 86 ⊙
Mon–Sat 9–12, 2–6, Sun 2–6

NICE

ALZIARI

This old family shop presses its own olive oil and sells *olives de Nice* by the kilo.

✉ 14 rue Saint-François-de-Paule ☎ 04 93 85 76 92
🚌 All buses to Gare Routière

CAPRIOGLIO

Wine store in old Nice, to suit all purses, from *vin de table* (stored in big orange tanks) to the top *crus*.

✉ 16 rue de la Préfecture
☎ 04 93 85 66 57 🚌 All buses to Gare Routière

ESPUNO

One of France's best bakeries. Try the regional *fougasse*.

✉ 35 rue Droite ☎ 04 93 80 50 67 🚌 All buses

MAISON AUER

Nice's last traditional maker of crystallised fruits.

✉ 7 rue St-François-de-Paule
☎ 04 93 85 77 98;
www.masion-auer.com
🚌 All buses to Gare Routière

ST-PAUL-DE-VENCE

LA PETITE CAVE DE SAINT-PAUL

An authentic 14th-century cellar containing a choice selection of Provençal wines, including those produced in the surrounding vineyards.

✉ 7 rue de l'Etoile ☎ 04 93 32 59 54

LES TROIS ETOILES

Only local products are sold at this liquer and olive oil shop, where the enthusiastic owner will keep you supplied with samples.

✉ 7 place de la Mairie
☎ 04 93 32 79 68

ST-RÉMY-DE-PROVENCE

LA CAVE AUX FROMAGES

Cheeses from throughout France, including regional specialities.

✉ 1 place Hilaire ☎ 04 90 92 32 45

LE PETIT DUC

This old-fashioned sweet shop prides itself on its traditional recipes, which are made entirely without artificial additives or preservatives.

✉ 7 boulevard Victor Hugo
☎ 04 90 92 08 31;
www.petit-duc.com

ST-TROPEZ (GASSIN)

PETIT VILLAGE

Stocks the wines of the Mâitres Vignerons of St-Tropez.

✉ Carrefour de la Foux, Gassin
☎ 04 94 56 32 04

VAISON-LA-ROMAINE

LOU CANESTEOU

This is considered Vaison's best cheese shop, offering a wide choice of locally made *chèvre*, including *banon* (wrapped in oak leaves), *picadon* and *cachat*.

✉ 10 rue Raspail ☎ 04 90 36 31 30

DRINKING PASTIS

Ice cubes first, then pastis, then water – a hallowed trio for a great Provençal custom – the *apéritif*. There are many different ways to drink pastis – *noyé* (drowned) with lots of water, *en flanc*, thick and strong, with very little water or as a cocktail. Try the 'parrot' (with mint syrup), the 'tomato' (with grenadine) or the 'Moorish' (with a bitter almond syrup). *Santé*!

Art, Antiques & Books

BOOKS FOR TEA

Avignon booksellers certainly know how best to sell their books, accompanied by a good cup of tea and a pâtisserie! There's nothing more enjoyable than browsing through your newly purchased book over scones and cream on the sun-drenched patio of Shakespeare in Avignon.

AIX

LIBRAIRIE DE PROVENCE

Large bookshop with an excellent choice of regional travel, literature and culinary titles.

✉ 31 cours Mirabeau
☎ 04 42 26 07 23

YVES UNGARO

An Aladdin's cave of pictures and *objets d'art* at the heart of Aix's antiques quarter.

✉ 1 rue Jaubert ☎ 04 42 63 22 94

ARLES

ANTIQUITÉS MAURIN

A treasure trove of regional furniture, paintings and ceramics from the 17th to the 20th century. Worldwide shipping service available.

✉ 4 rue de Grille ☎ 04 90 96 51 57; www.antiquites-maurin.com

LIBRAIRIE ACTES SUD

The bookshop of Arles' Actes Sud publishing house, in Le Méjan, a lively arts complex with a bar, cinema, restaurant and record shop.

✉ 43 rue du Docteur-Fanton
☎ 04 90 49 56 77

AVIGNON

HERVÉ BAUM

Modern and antique, chic and rustic – objects for home and garden.

✉ 19 rue Petite Fusterie
☎ 04 90 86 37 66

SHAKESPEARE

A discount English bookshop and tea shop. Occasional readings and recitals too. (➤ panel).

✉ 155 rue Carreterie
☎ 04 90 27 38 50

LES BAUX

LE MAS DES CHEVALIERS

Traditional Provençal furniture and *objets d'art*.

✉ Vallon de la Fontaine
☎ 04 90 54 44 48

L'ISLE-SUR-LA-SORGUE

L'ISLE AUX BROCANTES

There are over 35 dealers here, with a wide variety of items, trading in an 'antique village' emporium.

✉ Passage du Pont, 7 avenue des 4-Otages ☎ 04 90 20 69 93

NICE

GALERIE FERRERO

Exponents of the Nice School – very modern and very expensive.

✉ 2 rue du Congrés
☎ 04 93 88 34 44; www.galerieferreiro.com 🚌 217

TOURETTE J

Antique clocks, watches and musical boxes have been Monsieur Tourette's speciality for over 30 years.

✉ 17 rue Lépante ☎ 04 93 92 92 88

ROUSSILLON

GALERIE DES OCRES

Gifts and paints in every imaginable shade of ochre from France's Grand Cañon (➤ 45).

✉ Le Castrum ☎ 04 90 05 62 99

Specialist Shops

AIX

CINÉ PHOTO PROVENCE
Photographic equipment, films and a quality development service.
✉ 20 rue Bédarrides
☎ 04 42 93 47 30

ANTIBES

ANTIBES SHIPSERVICES
Here you will find everything from 'boaty' keyrings to fashionable yachting gear.
✉ 12–13 boulevard Aquillon
☎ 04 93 34 68 00;
www.antibes-ship.com

AVIGNON

PAPIERS-PLUMES
Papiers-Plumes sells beautiful pens, paper and desk objects for lovers of the art of letter writing.
✉ 45 rue Joseph-Vernet
☎ 04 90 82 68 77

SCENES INTERIEURES
Beautiful yet affordable interior design shop.
✉ 79 rue Bonneterie
☎ 04 90 86 46 31

CANNES

GENEVIÈVE LETHU
A delightful gift shop, crammed from floor to ceiling with original presents.
✉ 10 rue Maréchal-Joffre
☎ 04 93 68 18 19

MÉLONIE
The most exquisite dried flower arrangements you are ever likely to see.
✉ 80 rue d'Antibes
☎ 04 93 68 60 60

NICE

L'ATELIER DES JOUETS
A magical shop full of sturdy, educational toys and games in wood, metal and cloth. Ideal for children's gifts.
✉ 1 place de l'Ancien-Sénat
☎ 04 93 13 09 60 🚌 All buses to Gare Routière

HALOGENE
Trendy interior design store. Furniture, lighting and gift ideas.
✉ 21–23 rue de la Buffa
☎ 04 93 88 96 26 🚌 3, 7, 8, 9, 10, 14, 22, 52, 94

ST-PAUL-DE-VENCE

GAULT MINIATURES
Build you own Provençal village with these miniature houses beautifully crafted by Jean-Pierre Gault.
✉ 41 place de la Fontaine
☎ 04 93 32 50 54

HERBIER DE PROVENCE
You can't help but be drawn to the fragrant smell wafting from inside this shop – a pot-pourri of locally made herbs.
✉ Saint-Paul-de-Vence
☎ 04 93 32 91 51

ST-RÉMY-EN-PROVENCE

GALERIE GÉRARD SIOEN
Browse through arty photos, framed pictures, posters and cards of Provence.
✉ 55 rue Carnot ☎ 04 90 92 36 47; www.sioen-photo.com

A LITTLE-KNOWN WINE

Few people know about the tiny AOC (*appellation d'origine contrôllée*) wine region of Bellet near Nice, largely because the majority of the 160,000 or so bottles produced each year never gets any further than the cellars of the Riviera's top restaurants. The full-bodied red, with its wild cherry bouquet, can be aged up to 30 years. The golden white wine is reminiscent of Chablis and locals swear the rosé is the best accompaniment to regional fish dishes.

Casinos, Cinemas & Nightspots

THE MAN WHO BROKE THE BANK

The glitz of the Riviera's casinos is famous the world over, in particular the one at Monte-Carlo (▶ 39), where Charles Deville Wells turned $400 into $40,000 in a three-day gambling spree, thereby inspiring the song *The Man who Broke the Bank at Monte-Carlo*.

AIX-EN-PROVENCE

LE MISTRAL
Join the locals for the latest sounds in techno, house and garage music. Overflowingly popular nightclub.
✉ 3 rue Fréderic-Mistral
☎ 04 42 38 16 49
🕐 11pm–6am

LE SCAT
A traditional club, with live jazz, soul, rhythm and blues and reggae.
✉ 11 rue de la Verrerie
☎ 04 42 23 00 23;
🕐 Tue–Sat 11pm–5am

ANTIBES

LA SIESTA
One of the Côte d'Azur's most exotic nightclubs, with open-air dance floors, fountains, flaming torches and a wave-shaped casino.
✉ Route du Bord-de-la-Mer (between Antibes and la Brague)
☎ 04 93 33 31 31;
www.lasiesta.fr 🕐 Mid-May to mid-Sep 10pm–4am

ARLES

CAFÉ LA NUIT
Popular meeting place at the heart of Arles and subject of a famous van Gogh painting.
✉ 11 place du Forum ☎ 04 90 49 83 30 🕐 9am–midnight

AVIGNON

BAR LES CELESTINS
This tiny, brightly coloured bar draws a trendy crowd to its shady terrace for cocktails and barrelled beers.
✉ 38 place des Corps-Saints
☎ No telephone 🕐 7am–1am

PENICHE DOLPHIN BLUES
A café-theatre on a barge moored on the Rhône near Avignon's bridge. Cabaret and live music most evenings and a children's theatre during the day.
✉ Chemin de l'Île-Piot
☎ 04 90 82 46 96

UTOPIA/AJMI
Several screens showing original-version films, attached to Ajmi Jazz Club. Dance spectacles and cabaret.
✉ 4 rue Escaliers Sainte-Anne
☎ 04 90 82 65 36 (Ajmi 04 90 86 08 61; www.jazzalaymi.com) 🕐 Films daily. Jazz nights: Sun, Fri

JUAN-LES-PINS

WHISKEY À GOGO
Join locals for the latest sounds in this popular nightclub.
✉ Rue Jacques Leonetti
☎ 04 93 61 26 40 🕐 10pm–late summer only

MARSEILLE

TROLLEYBUS
Marseille's number one rock venue. Four themed performance bars.
✉ 24 quai Rive-Neuve ☎ 04 91 54 30 45; www.letrolley.com 🕐 Closed Sun–Wed 🚇 Metro (Vieux Port)

MONACO

CAFÉ DE PARIS
Even if you are not a big-spender you will be tempted by the dazzling array of slot machines in this famous café (▶ panel).

✉ Place du Casino ☎ 0377 92 16 20 00 🕐 All day from 10am

LE CASINO
The most famous, ritziest casino on the Riviera, but with an entrance fee.
✉ Place du Casino ☎ 0377 92 16 20 00; www.casino-monte-carlo.com 🕐 Mon–Fri from 2pm, Sat–Sun from noon
❓ Dress code

CINEMA D'ÉTÉ
An open-air cinema, summertime only.
✉ Chemin des Pêcheurs ☎ 0377 93 25 86 80

JIMMY'Z
Join the jet set at the chic-est disco on the Riviera.
✉ 26 avenue Princesse-Grace ☎ 0377 98 06 70 68 🕐 11.30pm–around 5am

NICE

AMBASSADE
Come dressed to the nines, grab a cocktail and hit the dance floor for great music and dancing with a sophisticated crowd. The decor is colourful, high-tech – one of the most beautiful nightclubs on the Riviera.
✉ 18 rue de Congrés ☎ 04 93 87 95 87 🕐 Wed–Sat 11pm–5am 🚌 11, 52, 59, 94, 98

CASINO RUHL
Nice's glamorous casino offers spectacular dinner cabarets as well as private gaming rooms.
✉ Promenade des Anglais ☎ 04 97 03 12 51; www.lucienbarriere.com 🕐 10am–dawn 🚌 59, 62, 60, 94, 217

CINÉMATHÈQUE
Classic films as well as the latest releases.
✉ 3 esplanade Kennedy ☎ 04 92 04 06 66 🕐 Tel for details 🚌 All buses to Gare Routière

LE GRAND ESCURIAL
Nice's largest indoor nightclub draws crowds of all ages for its guest DJs and popular sounds, ranging from house to R&B. Free breakfast is served at 4am.
✉ 29 rue Alphonse Karr ☎ 04 93 82 37 66 🕐 11pm–4am 🚌 38

GUEST
Night spot on the old port; dance floor for poseurs.
✉ 5 quai des Deux-Emmanuel ☎ 04 93 56 83 83 🕐 11.30pm–5am 🚌 9, 20

THOR PUB
A lively tourist pub and pavement terrace on Nice's main market square. Live music 10pm–2am nightly.
✉ 32 Cours Saleya ☎ 04 93 62 49 90; www.thor-pub.com 🕐 5.30pm–2.30am 🚌 All buses to Gare Routière

ST-TROPEZ

LES CAVES DU ROY
Reputedly St-Tropez's spiciest nightspot.
✉ Hôtel Byblos, avenue Paul-Signac ☎ 04 94 97 16 02 🕐 Easter–Oct 11pm–5am

VIP ROOM
This star-studded nightclub is the place to see and be seen.
✉ Boulevard 11-Novembre 1918 ☎ 04 94 97 14 70; www.viproom.fr 🕐 Mon–Wed

CAFÉ DE PARIS
This beautifully renovated art deco triumph contains a restaurant, as well as a gaming house, which in its heyday attracted the world's society. Ladies' man Edward VII was a frequent visitor, and the delicious dessert crêpe Suzette was created here, named after one of his companions.

Theatre, Opera & Classical Music

NICE'S ACROPOLIS

Love it or hate it, one thing is for sure – you can't ignore this monstrous mass of smoked glass and concrete slabs at the very hub of modern Nice. Its four high-tech auditoria, concert hall, bowling alley, exhibition halls, Cinémathèque (▶ 81) and extensive conference facilities are a major attraction in the city.

AIX

THÉÂTRE DU JEU DE PAUME
Aix's number one theatre and concert venue.
✉ 17–21 rue de l'Opera
☎ 04 42 99 12 00;
www.lestheatres.net

AVIGNON

THÉÂTRE DU CHÊNE-NOIR
Small theatre with a top repertory company.
✉ 8 bis rue Ste-Catherine
☎ 04 90 82 40 57;
www.theatreduchenenoir.asso.fr

MARSEILLE

MASSALIA THÉÂTRE
France's first marionnette theatre (▶ 58).
✉ 41 rue Jobin ☎ 04 95 04 95 70; www.theatremassalia.com

L'OPÉRA DE MARSEILLE
Predominantly Italian opera is performed here.
✉ 2 place Reyer
☎ 04 91 55 11 10;
www.opera.mariemarseille.fr
🚇 Metro (Vieux Port)

THÉÂTRE NATIONAL DE MARSEILLE LA CRIÉE
Marseille's leading theatre, housed in a former fish auction house, giving widely acclaimed performances.
✉ 30 quai de Rive-Neuve
☎ 04 91 54 70 54 🚌 31 33, 34, 41, 80, 81

NICE

L'ACROPOLIS
This vast, modern congress, arts and tourism centre is popular for theatre, films and concerts (▶ panel).
✉ 1 esplanade Kennedy
☎ 04 93 92 83 00;
www.nice-acropolis.com
🚌 All buses to Gare Routière

OPÉRA DE NICE
Home of the Nice Opera, the Philharmonic Orchestra and Ballet Corps, a rococo extravaganza in red and gold, modelled on the Naples opera house.
✉ 4/6 rue St-François-de-Paule
☎ 04 92 17 40 00;
www.opera-nice.org
🚌 All buses to Gare Routière

THÉÂTRE DE NICE (TDN)
Modern theatre presenting world-class shows.
✉ Promenade des Arts
☎ 04 93 13 90 90
🚌 All buses to Gare Routière

ORANGE

THÉÂTRE ANTIQUE
Concerts, opera and theatre in a superb setting (▶ 47).
✉ 47 rue Madeleine Roch
☎ 04 90 51 17 60;
www.theatre-orange.com

TICKET SALES

FNAC
✉ 19 rue de la République, Avignon ☎ 04 90 14 35 49

FNAC
✉ Centre Commercial Borse, Marseille ☎ 04 91 90 77 53

VIRGIN MEGASTORE
✉ 75 rue St-Ferréol, Marseille
☎ 04 91 55 55 00

FNAC
✉ Nice Etoile, 30 avenue Jean-Médecin, Nice ☎ 04 92 17 77 02

Participatory Sports

ALPINE/CROSS-COUNTRY SKIING

GAP BAYARD
One of the largest *ski-de-fond* (cross-country skiing) regions in the Hautes-Alpes.
☎ Tourist office 04 92 52 56 56; www.ville-gap.fr

ISOLA 2000
Isola is 90km north of Nice, from where you can take a day trip from Nice coach station, which includes a ski pass.
☎ Tourist office 04 93 23 15 15; www.isola2000.com

SERRE CHEVALIER
Provence's premier ski resort, near Briançon.
☎ Tourist office 04 92 24 98 98; www.serrechevalier.com

BALLOONING

MONTGOLFIÈRE PROVENCE
The ultimate way to explore the region of the Lubéron.
✉ Joucas ☎ 04 90 05 76 77; www.montegolfiere-provence-balloning.com

CANOEING

KAYAK VERT
The scenic Sorgue river is a favourite venue for canoeing and kayaking enthusiasts.
✉ 84800 Fontaine-de-Vaucluse
☎ 04 90 20 35 44;
www. canoe-fience.com

DEEP-SEA FISHING

GUIGO MARINE
Tired of lazing on the beach? At Guigo Marine you can book a day trip out at sea.
✉ 9 avenue 11-Novembre, Antibes ☎ 04 93 34 17 17; www.guigomarine.com
⏰ Jun–Oct

GOLF

ROYAL MOUGINS GOLF CLUB
To some, the best golf club on the Côte d'Azur.
✉ 424 avenue du Roi , Mougins ☎ 04 92 92 49 69; www.royalmougins.fr

RIVER CRUISES

MIREIO
Explore the Provençal waterways aboard the *Mireio*.
✉ Allée de l'Oulle, Avignon
☎ 04 90 85 62 25

SCUBA DIVING

FÉDÉRATION FRANÇAISE DE SPORTS SOUS-MARINS
The Riviera offers some of the finest diving in Europe.
✉ 24 quai Rive Neuve, Marseille ⏰ 04 91 33 99 31; www.ffessm.fr

TENNIS

LAWN TENNIS CLUB
Venue of the Nice Open and former club of French tennis star Yannick Noah.
✉ 5 avenue Suzanne-Lenguen, Nice ☎ 04 92 15 58 00; www.nicewltc.com

YACHT CHARTER

MOORINGS, NICE
Skippered yachts for hire.
✉ Quai Amiral-Infernet
☎ 04 92 00 42 22

SPECTATOR SPORTS

The region's number one spectator sport is *le foot* (football) and its top team is Olympique de Marseille, (☎ 04 91 32 13 21 for tickets). In the Camargue area, the most popular sport is bullfighting, but the Monte-Carlo Rally (Jan), Monaco's Formula One Grand Prix (May) and the Monte-Carlo Open Tennis Championships (Apr) are also huge crowd-pullers, along with regular horse-racing at Cagnes and Marseilles. All France is fanatical about cycling, with the Tour de France scaling some of Provence's highest mountain passes. Also, every summer crowds flock to Nice for its international triathlon (cycling, running, swimming) – the so-called 'Madman's Promenade'.

PROVENCE &
THE CÔTE D'AZUR
practical matters

WHAT YOU NEED

		UK	Germany	USA	Netherlands	Spain
● Required ○ Suggested ▲ Not required	Some countries require a passport to remain valid for a minimum period (usually at least six months) beyond the date of entry – contact their consulate or embassy or your travel agent for details.					
Passport/National Identity Card		●	●	●	●	●
Visa (regulations can change – check before you travel)		▲	▲	▲	▲	▲
Onward or Return Ticket		▲	▲	▲	▲	▲
Health Inoculations		▲	▲	▲	▲	▲
Health Documentation (reciprocal agreement document: ➤ 90, Health)		●	●	▲	●	●
Travel Insurance		○	○	○	○	○
Driving Licence (national with French translation or International)		●	●	●	●	●
Car Insurance Certificate (if own car)		○	○	○	○	○
Car Registration Document (if own car)		●	●	●	●	●

WHEN TO GO

Provence/Côte d'Azur

■ High season
▬ Low season

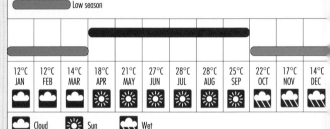

12°C JAN	12°C FEB	14°C MAR	18°C APR	21°C MAY	27°C JUN	28°C JUL	28°C AUG	25°C SEP	22°C OCT	17°C NOV	14°C DEC

☁ Cloud   ☀ Sun   🌧 Wet

TIME DIFFERENCES

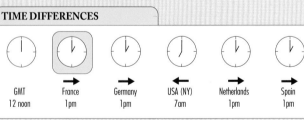

GMT 12 noon	France 1pm →	Germany 1pm →	USA (NY) 7am ←	Netherlands 1pm →	Spain 1pm →

TOURIST OFFICES

In the UK
French Government Tourist Office
178 Piccadilly, London W1J 9AL
☎ 09068 244123

Monaco Tourist Convention Office
7 Upper Grosvenor Street, London
W1K 2LX ☎ 0207 491 4264

In the USA
French Government Tourist Office
444 Madison Avenue, 16th floor
New York, NY10022
☎ 212/838 7800

Monaco Government Tourist
Bureau
565 Fifth Avenue, 23rd floor,
New York, NY10017
☎ 212/286 3330

ARRIVING

The national airline, Air France (www.airfrance.co.uk) has scheduled flights from Britain, mainland Europe and beyond to Marseille and Nice. French Railways (SNCF) operate high-speed trains (TGV) from Paris to main Provence and Côte d'Azur stations.

Marseille-Provence Airport
Kilometres to city centre

25 kilometres

Journey times	
	N/A
	25 minutes
	30 minutes

Nice-Côte d'Azur Airport
Kilometres to city centre

7 kilometres

Journey times	
N/A	
20 minutes	
15 minutes	

MONEY

The euro (€) is the official currency of France and Monaco. Banknotes are in denominatins of 5, 10, 20, 50, 100, 200 and 500 euros and coins are in denominations of 1, 2, 5, 10, 20 and 50 cents, and 1 and 2 euros. Euro traveller's cheques are widely accepted, as are major credit cards.

Credit and debit cards can also be used for withdrawing euro notes from cash machines, which are widely accessible.

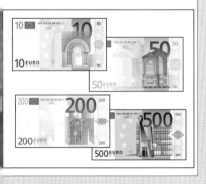

TIME

 France is one hour ahead of Greenwich Mean Time (GMT+1). From late March, when clocks are put forward one hour, until late October, French summer time (GMT+2) operates.

CUSTOMS

 YES

From another EU country for personal use (guidelines)
800 cigarettes, 200 cigars, 1 kilogram of tobacco
10 litres of spirits (over 22%)
20 litres of aperitifs
90 litres of wine, of which 60 litres can be sparkling wine
110 litres of beer

From a non-EU country for your personal use, the allowances are:
200 cigarettes OR
50 cigars OR
250 grams of tobacco
1 litre of spirits (over 22%)
2 litres of intermediary products (eg sherry) and sparkling wine
2 litres of still wine
50 grams of perfume
0.25 litres of eau de toilette
The value limit for goods is €175

Travellers under 17 years of age are not entitled to the tobacco and alcohol allowances.

 NO

Drugs, firearms, ammunition, offensive weapons, obscene material, unlicensed animals.

CONSULATES

UK
☎ 04 91 15 72 10
(Marseille)

Germany
☎ 04 93 83 55 25
(Nice);
377 97 77 51 53
(Monaco)

USA
☎ 04 91 54 92 00
(Marseille);
04 93 88 89 55
(Nice)

Netherlands
☎ 04 93 87 52 94
(Nice);
377 92 05 15 02
(Monaco)

TOURIST OFFICES

Provence and Côte d'Azur
● Comité Régional de Tourisme Provence-Alpes-Côte-d'Azur
Les Docks, 10 place de la Joliette, 13567 Marseille
☎ 04 91 56 47 00;
fax 04 91 56 47 01

Département Offices
● Comité Régional de Tourisme Riviéra Côte d'Azur
400 promenade des Anglais BP 3126, 06203 Nice
☎ 04 93 37 78 78; fax 04 93 86 01 06; www.guideriviera.com

● Comité Départemental du Tourisme des Bouches-du-Rhône
Le Montesquieu, 13 rue Roux de Brignoles, 13006 Marseille
☎ 04 91 13 84 13; fax 04 91 33 01 82; www.visitprovence.com

● Comité Départemental du Tourisme du Vaucluse
12 rue College-de-la-Croix BP147, 84008 Avignon
☎ 04 90 80 47 00; fax 04 90 86 86 08; www.provenceguide.com

● Comité Départemental du Tourisme du Alpes de Haute-Provence
Immeuble François Mitterrand BP170, 04006 Dignes-les-Bains
☎ 04 92 31 57 29; fax 04 92 32 24 94; www.aples-haute-provence.com

Monaco
● Office National du Tourisme de la Principauté de Monaco
2A boulevard des Moulins Monte-Carlo MC 98030 Monaco
☎ 377 92 16 61 66;
fax 377 92 16 60 00

Look for in the gazetteer for information in other towns and villages

NATIONAL HOLIDAYS

J	F	M	A	M	J	J	A	S	O	N	D
2		(2)	(2)	2(4)	1(3)	1	1			3	2

1 Jan	New Year's Day
27 Jan	St Devote's Day (Monaco only)
Mar/Apr	Easter Sunday and Monday
1 May	Labour Day
8 May	VE Day (France only)
May/Jun	Whit Sunday and Monday
June	Corpus Christi (Monaco only)
14 July	Bastille Day (France only)
15 Aug	Assumption
1 Nov	All Saints' Day
11 Nov	Remembrance Day (France only)
19 Nov	Monaco National Holiday (Monaco only)
9 Dec	Immaculate Conception (Monaco only)
25 Dec	Christmas Day

OPENING HOURS

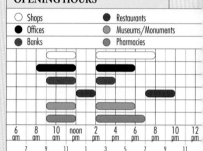

In addition to the times shown above, most shops close Sunday and many on Monday. Small food shops usually open from 7am and may open Sunday morning. Large department stores do not close for lunch and hypermarkets open 10am to 9 or 10pm, but may shut Monday morning. Banks are closed Sunday, as well as Saturday or Monday.
Museums and monuments have extended summer hours. Many close one day a week; either Monday (municipal ones) or Tuesday (national ones).

ELECTRICITY

The local power supply is: 220 volts

Type of socket: round two-hole sockets taking two-round-pin (or occasionally three-round-pin plugs. British visitors should bring an adaptor; US visitors a voltage transformer.

TIPS/GRATUITIES

Yes ✓ No ✗		
Restaurants (service included; tip optional)	✗	
Cafés (service included; tip optional)	✗	
Hotels (service included; tip optional)	✗	
Hairdressers	✓	€1
Taxis	✓	€1
Tour Guides	✓	€1
Cinema Usherettes	✓	30 cents
Porters	✓	€1
Restroom attendants	✓	30 cents
Toilets	✓	10 cents

PUBLIC TRANSPORT

 Internal Flights Air Inter – information via Air France (▶ 87, Arriving) and travel agents – is the French internal airline, linking 45 cities and towns, among them Marseille, Toulon, Avignon, Nîmes, Nice, Cannes and Fréjus. Some private airlines serve smaller towns.

 Area Buses Services run by a number of private companies are punctual and comfortable, but not very frequent outside main urban areas and coastal resorts. There are also SNCF buses, which serve places on rail routes where trains do not stop. Bus stations: Marseille (☎ 04 91 08 16 40); Nice (☎ 0892 701 206).

 Trains The main line in Provence and the Côte d'Azur links the towns and cities of the coast with the Rhône valley, with Marseille as its hub. A spectacular stretch runs behind the coast from Fréjus/St-Raphaël to Menton, which in summer is the most efficient way to move along the coast.

 Island Ferries There are ferries to the three islands off the coast of Hyères: the Îles d'Hyères (Porquerolles, Port-Cros and Ile de Levant) from five ports along the Côte d'Azur (Cavalaire, le Lavandou, Hyères-Plage, Toulon and la Tour-Fondue). Some services operate summer only.

 Urban Transport Most sizeable towns have a bus station (gare routière), often near the railway station. The most efficient bus network is in Nice, where computerised signboards at every bus stop inform you of the exact time of arrival of your service.

CAR RENTAL

 All the main car-rental companies have desks at Marseille and Nice airports and in main towns. Car rental is expensive, but airlines and tour operators offer fly-drive, and French Railways (SNCF) train-car packages, often more economical than renting locally.

TAXIS

 Taxis are very expensive and not allowed to cruise. They must pick up at ranks (stations de taxi) found at airports, railway stations and elsewhere. Always check there is a meter. There is a pick-up charge plus a rate per minute – check with the driver.

CONCESSIONS

Students/Youths Budget accommodation is available in dormitory rooms in youth hostels (Auberges de Jeunesse) in most towns; contact your home branch of the International Youth Hostel Federation (IYHF) or the Fédération Unie des Auberges de Jeunesse (☎ 01 44 89 87 27).

Senior Citizens A number of tour companies offer special arrangements for senior citizens; for further information contact the French Government Tourist Office (▶ 86, Tourist Offices). Senior citizens (aged over 60) are eligible for reduced or free entrance to sights, and if aged over 65 are eligible for fare discounts on public transport.

DRIVING

 Speed limits on toll motorways: 130kph (110kph when wet); non-toll motorways and dual carriageways: 110kph (100kph when wet). In fog (visibility less than 50m): 50kph all roads.

 Speed limits on country roads: 90kph (80kph when wet).

 Speed limits on urban roads: 50kph (limit starts at town sign).

 Must be worn in front seats at all times and in rear seats where fitted.

 Random breath-testing is frequent. Never drive under the influence of alcohol.

 Petrol, including unleaded (sans plomb) and diesel, are widely available. Petrol stations are numerous along main roads, but rarer in mountain areas. Some minor roads are closed on Sundays. Maps showing petrol stations are available from main tourist offices.

 A red warning triangle must be carried if your car has no hazard warning lights, but it is advised for all motorists. Place this 30m behind the car in the event of an accident or breakdown. On motorways ring emergency phones (every 2km) to contact the breakdown service. Off motorways, police will advise on local breakdown services.

PHOTOGRAPHY

 What to photograph: From the snow-peaked lower Alps to the Grand Cañon of central Provence and the calanques. The bright Provence light further enhances the beauty of the landscape.
Where to buy: Most popular brands and types of film and digital cards can be bought from shops and photo laboratories. Film development is expensive.
Restrictions: Some museums will allow you to photograph inside. In churches with frescoes and icons, prior permission for flashlight is required.

PERSONAL SAFETY

The Police Municipale (blue uniforms) carry out police duties in cities and towns. The Gendarmes (blue trousers, black jackets, white belts), the national police force, cover the countryside and smaller places. The CRS deal with emergencies and also look after safety on beaches. Monaco has its own police. To avoid danger or theft:

● Do not use unmanned roadside rest areas at night.
● Cars, especially foreign cars, should be secured.
● Beware of pickpockets.

Police assistance:
☎ **17**
from any call box

TELEPHONES

All telephone numbers in France comprise ten digits (eight in Monaco). There are no area codes except for Monaco (377 precedes number when phoning from outside the principality). Most public phones use a phone card (*télécarte*), sold in units of 50 or 120 in post offices, tobacconists and newsagents.

International Dialling Codes	
From France to:	
UK:	00 44
Germany:	00 49
USA:	00 1
Netherlands:	00 31
Spain:	0034

POST

Post Offices
Formerly the PTT (*Poste et Télécommunications*), La Poste deals with mail and telephone services. Outside main centres, post offices open shorter hours and may close 12–2. Letter boxes are yellow.
🕐 9–7 (12 Sat), closed Sun
☎ 04 91 15 47 00 (Marseille)
☎ 04 93 82 65 22 (Nice)

HEALTH

Insurance
EU nationals can obtain medical treatment at reduced cost on production of a qualifying card (EHIC for Britons); however this does not apply to Monaco. Private medical insurance is still advisable for all visitors to France.

Dental Services
As for general medical treatment, nationals of EU countries can obtain dental treatment at reduced cost. Around 70 per cent of dentists' standard fees are refunded. Private medical insurance is still advisable for all.

Sun Advice
The sunshine yearly average is 2,500 hours, rising to 3,000 hours along the coast. Summer, particularly July and August, is dry and hot. If walking, wear a hat and drink plenty of fluids. On the beach, a high-protection sunblock is a must.

Drugs
Pharmacies – recognised by their green cross sign – possess highly qualified staff able to offer medical advice, provide first aid and prescribe and provide a wide range of drugs, though some are available by prescription (*ordonnance*) only.

Safe Water
It is safe to drink tap water served in hotels and restaurants, but never drink from a tap marked *eau non potable*. Many prefer the taste of bottled water, which is cheap and widely available.

LANGUAGE

French is the native language. In Monaco, the traditional Monégasque language (a mixture of French, Provençal and Italian Ligurian) is spoken by the older generation. English is spoken by those involved in tourism and in the larger cosmopolitan centres – less so in smaller, rural places. However, attempts to speak French will always be appreciated. Below are some helpful words.
More extensive coverage can be found in the AA's Essential French Phrase Book.

hotel	l'hôtel	rate	le tarif
room	la chambre	breakfast	le petit déjeuner
single room	une personne	toilet	les toilettes
double room	deux personnes	bathroom	une salle de bain
per person	par personne	shower	une douche
per room	par chambre	key	la clé
one/two nights	une/deux nuits	chambermaid	la femme de chambre
reservation	une réservation		

bank	une banque	banknote	un billet
exchange office	un bureau de change	change	la monnaie
post office	la poste	credit card	une carte de crédit
foreign exchange	le change extérieur	traveller's cheque	un chèque de voyage
British pound	la livre sterling	exchange rate	le taux de change
American dollar	le dollar		

restaurant	le restaurant	starter	le hors d'oeuvres
café	la café	main course	le plat principal
table	une table	dish of the day	le plat du jour
menu	le menu	dessert	le dessert
set menu	le menu du jour	drink(s)	une (les) boisson
wine list	la carte des vins	waiter	le garçon
lunch	le déjeuner	waitress	la serveuse
dinner	le dîner	the bill	l'addition

aeroplane	l'avion	ticket	un billet
airport	l'aéroport	single/return	simple/retour
train	le train	ticket office	le guichet
train station	la gare	timetable	l'horaire
bus	l'autobus	seat	une place
bus station	la gare routière	non smoking	non-fumeurs
ferry/boat	le bateau	reserved	réservée
port	le port	window	la fenêtre

yes	oui	tomorrow	demain
no	non	yesterday	hier
please	s'il vous-plaît	how much?	combien?
thank you	merci	too expensive	trop cher
hello	bonjour	open	ouvert
goodbye	au revoir	closed	fermé
good evening	bonsoir	second class	deuxième classe
sorry	pardon	first class	première classe
excuse me	excusez-moi	you're welcome	de rien/avec plaisir
help!	au secours!	okay	d'accord
today	aujourd'hui	I don't know	Je ne sais pas

REMEMBER

- Contact the airport or airline on the day prior to leaving to ensure that the flight details are unchanged, and check in two hours before your flight time to allow for extra security checks.
- Expect to pay an airport departure tax (usually already included in the price of your flight ticket).
- Check the duty-free limits of the country you are entering before departure.

Index

TwinPack
Provence & the Côte d'Azur

Written by Teresa Fisher
Updated by Jackie Staddon and Hilary Weston
Produced by AA Publishing
Editorial management Apostrophe S Limited
Designer Jacqueline Bailey
Series editor Cathy Hatley

A CIP catalogue record for this book is available from the British Library.

ISBN 978-0-7495-5542-9

Published by AA Publishing, a trading name of Automobile Association Developments Limited, whose registered office is Fanum House, Basing View, Basingstoke, Hampshire, RG21 4EA. Registered number 1878835.

© AUTOMOBILE ASSOCIATION DEVELOPMENTS LIMITED 2008
First published 2008

Colour separation by Keenes, Andover
Printed and bound by Everbest Printing Co. Limited, China

ACKNOWLEDGEMENTS
The Automobile Association would like to thank the following photographers, companies and picture libraries for their assistance in the preparation of this book. Abbreviations for the picture credits are as follows – (t) top; (b) bottom; (c) centre; (l) left; (r) right; (AA) AA World Travel Library.

1 AA/A Baker; 5t AA/B Rieger; 5b AA/R Strange; 6 AA/C Sawyer; 7t AA/A Baker; 7b AA/R Strange; 9 AA/A Baker; 12t AA/C Sawyer; 12b AA/A Baker; 13t AA/C Sawyer; 13b AA/R Strange; 14 AA/R Strange; 15 AA/C Sawyer; 16 AA/C Sawyer; 17 AA/R Strange; 18 AA/A Baker; 19 AA/A Baker; 20t AA/R Strange; 20b AA/C Sawyer; 21t AA/R Strange; 21b AA/R Strange; 23t AA/R Strange; 23b AA/R Strange; 24t AA/R Strange; 24b AA/R Strange; 25t AA/C Sawyer; 25c AA/C Sawyer; 25b AA/C Sawyer; 26t AA/R Strange; 26b AA/C Sawyer; 27t AA/R Strange; 27b AA/R Strange; 28t AA/R Moore; 28b AA/R Strange; 29t AA/C Sawyer; 29b AA/C Sawyer; 30t AA/C Sawyer; 30b AA/R Strange; 31t AA/R Moore; 31b AA/A Baker; 32t AA/A Baker; 32b AA/R Strange; 33t AA/C Sawyer; 33b AA/C Sawyer; 34t AA/A Baker; 34b AA/A Baker; 35t AA/A Baker; 35b AA/R Strange; 36t AA/A Baker; 36b AA/C Sawyer; 37t AA/R Strange; 37b AA/C Sawyer; 38t AA/C Sawyer; 38b AA/C Sawyer; 39t AA/C Sawyer; 39b AA/A Baker; 40t AA/R Strange; 40b AA/C Sawyer; 41t AA/C Sawyer; 41b AA/R Strange; 42t AA/R Strange; 42b AA/C Sawyer; 43t AA/A Baker; 43b AA/A Baker; 44t AA/C Sawyer; 44b AA/R Strange; 45t AA/A Baker; 45b AA/A Baker; 46t AA/R Strange; 46b AA/C Sawyer; 47t AA/C Sawyer; 47b AA/R Strange; 48t AA/R Strange; 48b AA/R Strange; 49t AA/B Smith; 49b AA/A Baker; 50 AA/R Moore; 51 Musée de l'Arles et de la Provence antiques. Cl. M Lacanaud; 52 AA/C Sawyer; 53 AA/R Strange; 54 AA/A Baker; 55 AA/A Baker; 56 AA/N Ray; 57 AA/R Strange; 58 Musee de l'Automobiliste; 59 AA/N Sumner; 60t AA/A Baker; 60b AA/P Kenward; 61t AA/C Sawyer; 61b AA/C Sawyer; 84 AA/R Moore; 85t AA/A Baker; 85b AA/C Sawyer; 90l AA/M Jourdan; 90tr AA/R Moore; 90br AA/R Moore.
Front cover: Sunflower, AA/C Sawyer; Fountain, AA/R Strange; Seafood Platter, AA/P Kenward; Monte Carlo Casino, AA/A Baker; Herbs, Boat, Olive Oil, AA/C Sawyer.
Back Cover: Statue, AA/R Strange; Hats, Table setting, AA/C Sawyer; Casino, AA/J A Tims.

Every effort has been made to trace the copyright holders, and we apologise in advance for any accidental errors. We would be happy to apply the corrections in the following edition of this publication.

A03196
Maps in this title produced from mapping © MAIRDUMONT/Falk Verlag 2007

TITLES IN THE TWINPACK SERIES
• Algarve • Andalucía • Corfu • Costa Blanca • Costa Brava • Costa del Sol • Crete •
• Croatia • Cyprus • Dubai • Gran Canaria • Lanzarote & Fuerteventura • Madeira •
• Mallorca • Malta & Gozo • Menorca • Provence & the Côte d'Azur • Tenerife •

Dear **TwinPack** Traveller

Your comments, opinions and recommendations are very important to us. So please help us to improve our travel guides by taking a few minutes to complete this simple questionnaire.

You do not need a stamp (unless posted outside the UK). If you do not want to cut this page from your guide, then photocopy it or write your answers on a plain sheet of paper.

Send to: **The Editor, AA TwinPack Travel Guides, FREEPOST SCE 4598, Basingstoke RG21 4GY.**

Your recommendations…

We always encourage readers' recommendations for restaurants, nightlife or shopping – if your recommendation is used in the next edition of the guide, we will send you a *FREE* **AA TwinPack Guide** of your choice. Please state below the establishment name, location and your reasons for recommending it.

_____

_____

_____

_____

Please send me **AA TwinPack**

Algarve ❑ Andalucía ❑ Corfu ❑ Costa Blanca ❑
Costa Brava ❑ Costa del Sol ❑ Crete ❑ Croatia ❑
Cyprus ❑ Dubai ❑ Gran Canaria ❑ Lanzarote & Fuerteventura ❑
Madeira ❑ Mallorca ❑ Malta & Gozo ❑ Menorca ❑
Provence & the Côte d'Azur ❑ Tenerife ❑
(please tick as appropriate)

About this guide…

Which title did you buy?

AA *TwinPack* _____

Where did you buy it? _____

When? m m / y y

Why did you choose an AA *TwinPack Guide*? _____

_____

_____

_____

Did this guide meet your expectations?

Exceeded ❑ Met all ❑ Met most ❑ Fell below ❑

Please give your reasons _____

_____

_____

continued on next page…

Were there any aspects of this guide that you particularly liked? _____

_____

_____

Is there anything we could have done better? _____

_____

_____

About you...

Name *(Mr/Mrs/Ms)* _____

  Address _____

_____

  _____ Postcode _____

  Daytime tel no _____

Please only give us your mobile phone number if you wish to hear from us about other products and services from the AA and partners by text or mms.

Which age group are you in?

  Under 25 ❑   25–34 ❑   35–44 ❑   45–54 ❑   55–64 ❑   65+ ❑

How many trips do you make a year?

  None ❑   One ❑   Two ❑   Three or more ❑

Are you an AA member? Yes ❑   No ❑

About your trip...

When did you book? m m / y y   When did you travel? m m / y y

How long did you stay? _____

Was it for business or leisure? _____

Did you buy any other travel guides for your trip?

  If yes, which ones? _____

Thank you for taking the time to complete this questionnaire. Please send it to us as soon as possible, and remember, you do not need a stamp *(unless posted outside the UK)*.

Happy Holidays!